Advance Praise For
Powerdown

Powerdown is a fearless, no-holds-barred view of our prospects in the post fossil fuel world. Courageous, clear . . . essential reading.
— David Orr, author of *Earth in Mind, The Nature of Design* and *The Last Refuge*

In *Powerdown,* Heinberg confirms that the Party really is over as we enter the second half of the Age of Oil. He provides penetrating arguments to show why the ethic of growth at any cost has to end. He goes on to offer proposals for new politico-economic structures to ameliorate the tensions of the transition from growth to decline, and equip the survivors. The island at the end of the voyage turns out to be an attractive place of harmony and justice, but it is surrounded by some very rough seas. This book is essential reading.
— Colin J. Campbell, petroleum geologist, former oil executive, author of *The Coming Oil Crisis*

Richard Heinberg's *Powerdown* is a balanced hard-headed analysis of the politically unthinkable, the coming implosion of contemporary techno-industrial society. Heinberg's premise is simple: no factor has played a greater role in the explosive development of global civilization since the 19th Century than abundant cheap fossil energy but, while the human enterprise is committed to maintaining to its steep upward trajectory, the rocket is running out of fuel. *Powerdown* provides a visionary response to the coming energy famine, a clarion call to cooperative solutions based on the conviction that realism must trump self-delusion in matters of cultural survival.
— William E. Rees, PhD, author of *Our Ecological Footprint*

Here's a firm, humane, extraordinarily well-written assessment of
the likely realities of life after fossil fuels, soon to begin on
the planet nearest you. *Powerdown* is an essential read
if you care to understand the deep structure of the
coming Dark Age and to choose actions that will
become us as a species.
— Stephanie Mills, author of *Epicurean Simplicity*

Richard Heinberg is that rare combination of scholar
and visionary who is intellectually and emotionally unencumbered
enough to ask the toughest questions; and to reconcile
a truth which no one wants to believe with an emerging
world reality only a few are brave enough to see.
His compassion for mankind is obvious.
Whenever I need a reality check and to calibrate my
own compass on what Peak Oil means,
I check first with Richard Heinberg.
— Mike Ruppert, publisher/editor, www.fromthewilderness.com

Powerdown is the only sane response to the world's
increasingly grave problems of energy depletion, environmental
degradation, and over-population. Richard Heinberg
truly understands the nature, scale, and urgency of our global
situation. As we briefly rest on the plateau
of world oil production peak, Heinberg first outlines the
possible unpleasant paths our society may take through energy
decline. He then makes it devastatingly clear that a
humane post-carbon future depends on urging our
governments to powerdown, while we start to re-localize
our economies and build community lifeboats.
— Julian Darley, author of *High Noon for Natural Gas* and
founder of The Post Carbon Institute

POWER DOWN

OPTIONS AND ACTIONS FOR A POST-CARBON WORLD ▶

RICHARD HEINBERG

NEW SOCIETY PUBLISHERS

Cataloguing in Publication Data:
A catalog record for this publication is available from the National Library of
Canada.

Cover design by Diane McIntosh.
Cover Image: Bob Gomel, Time Life Pictures.

Printed in Canada by Friesens Inc.

Paperback ISBN: 0-86571-510-6

Inquiries regarding requests to reprint all or part of *Powerdown* should be
addressed to New Society Publishers at the address below.

To order directly from the publishers, please add $4.50 shipping to the price of
the first copy, and $1.00 for each additional copy (plus GST in Canada). Send
check or money order to:

New Society Publishers
P.O. Box 189, Gabriola Island, BC V0R 1X0, Canada
1-800-567-6772

New Society Publishers' mission is to publish books that contribute in fundamental ways to building an ecologically sustainable and just society, and to do
so with the least possible impact on the environment, in a manner that models
this vision. We are committed to doing this not just through education, but
through action. We are acting on our commitment to the world's remaining
ancient forests by phasing out our paper supply from ancient forests worldwide.
This book is one step towards ending global deforestation and climate change.
It is printed on acid-free paper that is **100% old growth forest-free** (100%
post-consumer recycled), processed chlorine free, and printed with vegetable
based, low VOC inks. For further information, or to browse our full list of
books and purchase securely, visit our website at: www.newsociety.com

NEW SOCIETY PUBLISHERS   www.newsociety.com

Power-down \ \ n. 1. the energy famine that engulfed industrial nations in the early 21st century 2. the deliberate process of cooperation, contraction, and conversion that enabled humanity to survive . . .

CONTENTS

ACKNOWLEDGMENTS

A few of the core ideas of this book emerged through an e-mail dialogue with John Michael Greer; thank you, John, for your brilliant suggestions. Other ideas herein were shaped by the ongoing dialogues of members of the Energy Resources newsgroup <energyresources@yahoo.com>.

Thanks also to my colleagues Julian Darley and Celine Rich Darley, with whom I have enjoyed collaborating on several projects related to the subject of this book; and to Paul Baer, who read the first three chapters and offered valuable comments.

I continue to appreciate the enthusiastic support of the staff at New Society Publishers, most notably that of Chris and Judith Plant, for their willingness to take on challenging and controversial material like this; and Ingrid Witvoet for her careful editorial work on the manuscript.

Thanks to my colleagues at New College of California, and especially to my students, who have patiently listened to me wrestle with the concepts in this book in my lectures.

And finally to my wife Janet Barocco, who found several of the chapter-opening quotes, and who tries ever valiantly to keep me grounded in the present.

INTRODUCTION

When I was a boy in the countryside — fifty years ago
and more — people [gardened] for self-sufficiency, for
it would not have occurred to them to do otherwise.
People were self-reliant because they had to be: it was a
way of life. They were doing what generations had done
before them; simply carrying on a traditional way of life.
Money was a rare commodity: far too valuable to be
spent on things you could grow or make yourself.
It was spent on tools or fabric for clothes or luxury foods
like tea or coffee. They would have laughed at a diet
of store-bought foods. . . .

—John Seymour, *The Self-Sufficient Gardener* (1979)

I am in the cabin of an MD80 jetliner en route from San Francisco to Dallas. It is night, and as I look out the airplane window I see a dense web of lights spread upon the darkened landscape. It is a beautiful sight, and yet a profoundly disturbing one. Aside from streetlamps, nearly every one of those tiny lights emanates from a house, or from a car crawling across the landscape.

Each tells an individual human story of struggle for survival and prosperity. And each is in some way connected back to a fossil-fuel energy source.

That source has its own story — one that began hundreds of millions of years ago, but that will end within the lifetime of children now living, as our fossil-fuel inheritance is burned once and for all. What will then happen to all of these lights — and to the lives to which they are tied?

It is a poignant thought, and an ironic one given the context in which it appears. I am looking out and down from the interior of a machine that is being forcibly thrust up into the sky — again by the burning of fossil fuels. The walls and fabrics that surround me are mostly made of fossil fuels. So too, to a large degree, is the computer on my lap.

As I think about my computer, the irony deepens. Just as I can look down from this airplane and take in a hundred square miles at a glance, I can take in information through my computer (when it is Internet-connected) and look down, as it were, on current events, human history, and human cultural geography as few humans could have hoped to do only decades ago.

And what a view one gets from this information pinnacle! A century ago our recent ancestors were riding in horse-drawn carts; today we have photos taken from the surface of Mars. We have landed humans on the Moon. We have covered huge expanses of our planet with seas of concrete on which to drive and park our billion cars. We have built skyscrapers and diverted great rivers. There are roughly as many humans alive now as existed cumulatively throughout all of the millennia prior to the Industrial Revolution. That means that a large proportion of all of the geniuses — and monsters — who have ever lived are alive today. And whenever one of these extraordinary individuals does something, we can hear about it instantly via our global communications networks.

Most of this edifice of modernity has been constructed within a single human lifetime: I still occasionally speak with people who can recall seeing the first automobile arrive in their town. And we are seeing the brief flowering of industrialism, in all its magnificence, with our own eyes, in real time. What a show!

But that's not all we see.

We have climbed very high, but also very far out on a spindly ecological limb. We may live, as Paul Simon once put it, in "an age of miracles and wonders," but we also live in a time in which several "storms" are colliding, as in the book and movie *The Perfect Storm:*

- **Resource depletion:** From the standpoint of the global economy, probably the most immediate threat comes from the depletion of fossil fuels (both oil and, in North America and Britain, natural gas). But fresh water resources, wild oceanic fish stocks, phosphates (necessary for agriculture), and topsoil are also dwindling.
- **Continued population growth:** While the rate of global population growth shows signs of slowing, the total reached six billion in 1998, and in the six years since that time we have added an additional 400 million humans — nearly the population of North America.
- **Declining per-capita food production:** For nearly the entire 20th century, food production outpaced population growth. However, world grain harvests for the past five years reveal a frightening trend: it appears that the trajectory of per-capita grain production has leveled off and may be beginning to fall, probably for a variety of reasons (including loss of arable land to urbanization, fresh water shortages, and bad weather).
- **Global climate change and other signs of environmental degradation:** Agricultural civilizations have developed over just the past few thousand years — an eyeblink in geological time. This has been a period characterized by a relatively stable, benign global climatic regime. Now that regime appears to be coming to an end, almost certainly as the result of a human-induced enhancement of the atmospheric greenhouse effect. It is unclear whether civilization can persist in a less favorable and less stable climate, as food production could be

even further imperiled. If the world's sea levels rise significantly, as they are predicted to do as a result of the partial melting of polar ice, many coastal cities would be inundated. Moreover, concerns are now being raised that cold, fresh water from melting Greenland glaciers may halt the Gulf Stream and plunge Europe and much of North America into a new ice age.[1]

- **Unsustainable levels of US debt and a potential dollar collapse:** Since World War II, the world has relied on the US dollar as the basis for monetary stability. Increasingly, the US has taken advantage of this situation by running up ever-larger trade deficits and more foreign-financed government debt. The current level of American debt — internal and external — is unprecedented and unsustainable, and US Treasury officials have made efforts in 2003 and early 2004 to gently lower the value of the dollar in relation to other currencies. However, if the dollar is devalued too much, other nations (including China and Japan) may decide to cease investing their savings in American stocks and Treasury securities; this in turn could trigger a dollar collapse. In short, the global monetary system that has maintained relative stability for the past several decades appears to be fraying. Just when the nations of the world need to invest heavily in renewable energy systems, efficiency measures, and sustainable agricultural production in order to deal with problems previously mentioned, investment capital may disappear altogether in a global financial crisis.[2]

- **International political instability:** The recent declaration by the US that it has a right to preemptive war, and its use of that "right" as a rationale for its invasion of Iraq, could potentially plunge international affairs into a new era of lawlessness. Henceforth, an attack by any nation on any other could be justifiable as self-protection against imagined future threats. Meanwhile, the development and proliferation of new space-based, electronic, genetic, and micro-nuclear weapons opens the possibility for ever deadlier forms of warfare, of which some have the potential to wipe out entire ethnic populations or to render whole continents uninhabitable.

These problems are related to one another in complex, often mutually reinforcing ways. Taken together, they constitute the most severe challenge our species has ever faced. They represent not merely a likely culmination of human history; in their ongoing and potential environmental impacts, they also may collectively signal one of the most momentous events in all of geological time.

This confluence of unprecedented achievements and threats — which most of us have learned to take for granted as being the ordinary state of affairs for humanity — is overwhelming when one contemplates it *in toto*, as if seeing from above. But usually we see it only one bit at a time, and we prefer *not* to think about how the parts may combine into one terrible whole.

❖ ❖ ❖

Everyone knows the classic scene from a dozen Westerns: a self-reliant, grizzled geezer is taken to see a doctor, perhaps for the first time in his life. He knows the prognosis intuitively and is prepared for the worst. "Tell me the truth, Doc."

That's how some of us feel when we read about climate change or the ongoing degradation of the world's coral reefs. *Give it to me straight: I'd rather know than live in denial.*

But most of the leaders of government and industry feel differently. They are more like the character Colonel Jessup, played by Jack Nicholson, in *A Few Good Men* (1992). In that film's climactic courtroom scene, Lieutenant Kaffee (Tom Cruise), cross-examining Jessup, insists, "I want the truth." Jessup shouts back, "You can't handle the truth!"

Nor, it seems, can we — at least not in the estimation of the masters of the corporate media. And so we tend to receive only sanitized versions of the news about our world. Occasionally, disturbing information does appear on television or in the newspapers, but the offending story usually shows up buried in the same broadcast, or on the same page, as others about relatively ephemeral political developments, local murders, the lives of entertainment stars, or scores in sports games.

A recent example: on May 15, 2003, nearly every newspaper in the world headlined the disturbing results of a study published that day in the prestigious British science journal, *Nature*. In their article titled "Rapid worldwide depletion of predatory fish communities," Ransom A. Myers and Boris Worm had reported, "Our analysis suggests that the global ocean has lost more than 90 percent of large predatory fishes." Most of this depletion is attributable to the fishing industry. In many species, when populations are reduced beyond a certain point, recovery becomes impossible. Many fish species appear to be beyond, at, or close to that point of no return. With this news story, the world human community was effectively put on notice that the oceans may be dying.

That same day, other newspaper headlines included: "Menem Pulls Out of Argentina Race," and "Israeli Forces Kill Five in Gaza Raid." Argentinean politics and the ongoing Israeli occupation of Palestine certainly deserved whatever coverage they got that day, but how was the average reader to weigh the relative importance of the three news items? In the following days there were more headlines about the Argentinean elections, and about further violence in occupied Palestine. But the story about the oceans largely vanished from view, and it is likely that only a tiny percentage of the population understood its importance enough to go out of their way to seek out follow-up items during the following weeks and months. Most people likely did not notice, for example, an article by Richard Sadler and Geoffrey Lean titled "Fish Stocks and Sea Bird Numbers Plummet as Soaring Water Temperatures Kill Off Vital Plankton," published on October 19th of the same year in the British newspaper, *The Independent*. As a result of global warming, "the North Sea is undergoing 'ecological meltdown,'" the authors reported, according to startling new research. Scientists say that they are witnessing "a collapse in the system," with devastating implications for fisheries and wildlife. Record sea temperatures are killing off the plankton on which all life in the sea depends, because they underpin the entire marine food chain. Fish stocks and sea bird populations have slumped.[3]

On the day it was published, this story was generally drowned out by "Pope Beatifies Mother Teresa," and "Blair Back at Work after Heartbeat Scare." Perhaps the folks in charge are right: maybe we *can't* handle the truth (though it's nice to be given the chance). Most of us do seem to enjoy our pleasant illusions, after all.

We get plenty of help in this regard from the relentlessly cheery entertainment industry, but also from politicians of every stripe. Trying to tell the public truly awful news is considered impolite — unless it is news about something that can be blamed on an opposing political group or some foreign enemy. While leftists sometimes highlight certain ecological crises as a way of blaming corporations and right-wing governments, they often make sure to frame their complaints in a way that suggests that the problems can be solved by implementing a plan being put forward by liberal politicians or NGOs. Meanwhile, commentators on the political right revile "environmental alarmists" for allegedly exaggerating the seriousness of ecological dilemmas to suit their own ideological purposes.

So, as leftists make skewed and half-hearted attempts to discuss ecological crises, the attacks from the right have their intended chilling effect. Mainstream environmentalists these days often tend reflexively to pull their punches and temper their warnings. There are serious problems facing us, they say again and again, but if we just make the right choices those problems will painlessly vanish. When they are at their most baleful, environmental scientists tell us that we have the current decade in which to make fundamental changes; if we don't, then the slide into ecological ruin will be irreversible. On the first Earth Day we were told we had the decade of the 1970s in which to change course; but for the most part we didn't. Then we had the '80s . . . ditto. During the 1992 Earth Summit in Rio we heard that humanity had the '90s to reform itself; after that, there might be no turning back. There was still no fundamental change in direction, and here we are a dozen years on. I expect any day now to read an official pronouncement to the effect that we have the remainder of the first decade of the new century in which to make changes, *or else*. How many warnings do we get? Isn't it reasonable by now to assume that we are living on borrowed time?

The environmentalists' timidity about saying that we are past the expiration date on facile hope is understandable. No one wants to be viewed as Chicken Little. In *The Population Bomb* (1968), biologist Paul Ehrlich wrote that it was then already too late: "In the 1970s the world will undergo famines — hundreds of millions of people are going to starve to death in spite of any crash programs embarked upon now." Throughout the book, he made other specific — and, in retrospect, very unwise — forecasts. Of course, the Great Famine of the 1970s never happened. To be sure, millions of people starved during that decade, but not in a dramatic enough way to justify Ehrlich's Jeremiad. Ever since then, whenever an environmentalist releases a new time-stamped warning, some commentator chirps, "We've heard it before: those prophecies of doom are always wrong. Why should we listen now?" Most environmentalists are scientists, and scientists are accustomed to couching their assertions in cautious terms anyway. Add to this the Chicken Little factor, and one can hardly blame them for shying away from plain talk about the inevitable consequences of our present pattern of existence.

In his immediate predictions, Ehrlich was indeed mistaken. But in principle he was undeniably correct: if we don't voluntarily reverse human population growth, nature will do it for us.

During the past three decades, industrial civilization has managed to pull a rabbit out of a hat: food production mostly stayed ahead of population growth. We *seemed* to have dodged the bullet. But now, instead of the 3.5 billion humans who were around when *The Population Bomb* was published, we are 6.4 billion — a far larger target — and our ability to duck and weave is quickly waning. World per-capita grain production is falling and ecosystems are failing. Still, today almost no one talks about the need for population reduction in the courageous and straightforward way that Ehrlich did back in the late 1960s. No, we've learned to be more cautious and nuanced in our comments about the coming demographic holocaust.

❖ ❖ ❖

I cannot help but write precisely the kind of book that I myself would want to read. And I am one of those grizzled geezers who would rather know the truth, however alarming it may be. I can only trust that there will be others similarly inclined.

For the past couple of decades I have been a full-time independent information worker — a journalist, editor, newsletter publisher, researcher, and college professor. Though I teach a course in human ecology, I have no formal specialty: I am a generalist. My goal is simply to gain an accurate overview of what is happening in the world. In order to do this, I have had to learn how to prioritize information. I have developed the habit of asking, *what is the most important thing to know in order to understand this situation?* This effort to prioritize has led me to realize the crucial role of energy in ecosystems and human societies, and of fossil fuels in modern industrial societies. And this realization in turn led me to write my recent book, *The Party's Over: Oil, War and the Fate of Industrial Societies.* There, I recounted how the Industrial Revolution grew out of our increasing use of fossil fuels — first coal, then oil. I described the 20th century as the Petroleum Century, a one-time special event in human history. During this spectacular period, total global commercial energy production increased by about 9 times, and efficiency gains doubled that figure in terms of utilized energy, yielding an overall 18-fold rise in energy available to human beings. It was this energy windfall that enabled us to transform our way of life from oxcarts and Pony Express messengers to jetliners and cell phones. Meanwhile the human population quadrupled during the "century of progress" to take advantage of its unprecedented energy subsidy.

This was only the prologue to my real message, which was a pointed warning. We have always known in theory that fossil fuels are non-renewable, and are therefore finite in quantity. Now signs are appearing that the rate of global oil extraction may peak and begin to subside *within the next few years* as a result of geological conditions that cannot be altered by any expected technical advances in exploration or recovery. The consequences are likely to be calamitous. (Many of the most important ideas in *The Party's Over* are summarized and updated in Chapter 1.)

❖ ❖ ❖

By this time the reader has likely surmised that the purpose of this book is not to provide yet another cheerful manual on how to save the (human) world (as we know it). But neither is it my goal to helplessly bemoan our inevitable collective fate. Rather, it is to explore realistically our options for the next century. When I say "realistically," I mean that I take as my starting point the belief — arrived at reluctantly after years of reflection and study — that we have already advanced so far in certain directions as to have foreclosed possibilities that we would all prefer were available.

I take it as a given that we have already overshot Earth's long-term carrying capacity for humans — and have drawn down essential resources — to such an extent that some form of societal collapse is now inevitable. I intend the word "collapse" in a somewhat technical sense that is borrowed from the work of Joseph Tainter, author of *The Collapse of Complex Societies*.[4] Tainter defines "collapse" as a substantial reduction in social complexity. This can occur either relatively quickly and chaotically, or in a more gradual and managed fashion. In the best case, this would amount to a planned contraction, in which population levels and per-capita resource usage would be scaled back dramatically over decades.

But of course the word *collapse* is fraught with dire implications. Many of us tend to think of a civilization's collapse as being sudden and complete, but this has usually not tended to be the case in past instances — ancient Rome, Minoan Crete, the Western Chou Empire, and the like. Collapses of historical societies have usually occurred over a period of 100 to more than 500 years. Also, collapse may or may not result in the destruction of a society's primary institutions. Often it is difficult to pinpoint the exact moment of the commencement of collapse, and the process may be clearly under way only decades after the society in question has reached its pinnacle of extent and achievement (we will examine the process of collapse in more detail in Chapter 5).

In the present instance, we are already seeing the first phases of collapse, as signaled by the disruption of global climate, the decline of oceanic ecosystems, energy resource depletion, and the peaking of per-capita global grain production; however, it is unlikely that anyone now alive will see the end of the process. From a sufficiently distant temporal perspective, future historians will likely view the period from roughly 1800 to 2000 as the growth phase of industrial civilization, and the period from 2000 to 2100 or 2200 as its contraction or collapse phase.

Even if a reversal of growth is inevitable, the form it will take is as yet unclear, and will be determined by the actions of the present generation. We have weapons and other technological means to end human life forever. We also have the knowledge and skills necessary to build small-scale, decentralized, sustainable communities capable of providing a high level of human satisfaction and cultural attainment while degrading the environment to only a relatively minor extent over time.

THIS IS HOW I FEEL SOMETIMES

Imagine yourself in the following circumstance: You have just awakened from sleep to find yourself on a tarpaper raft floating away from shore. With you on the raft are a couple of hundred people, most of whom seem completely oblivious to their situation. They are drinking beer, barbecuing ribs, fishing, or sleeping. You look at the rickety vessel and say to yourself, "My God, this thing is going to sink any second!"

Miraculously, seconds go by and it is still afloat. You look around to see who's in charge. The only people you can find who appear to have any authority are some pompous-looking characters operating a gambling casino in the middle of the raft. In back of them stand heavily armed soldiers. You point out that the raft appears dangerous. They inform you that it is the safest and most wonderful vessel ever constructed, and that if you persist in suggesting otherwise the guards will exercise their brand of persuasion on you. You back away, smiling, and move to the edge of the raft. At this point, you're convinced (and even comment to a stranger next to you) that, with those idiots at the helm, the raft can't last more than another minute or so.

A minute goes by and still the damn thing is afloat. You turn your gaze out to the water. You notice now that the raft is surrounded by many sound-looking canoes, each carrying a family of indigenous fishers. Men on the raft are systematically forcing people out of the canoes and onto the raft at gunpoint, and shooting holes in the bottoms of the canoes. This is clearly insane behavior: the canoes are the only possible sources of escape or rescue if the raft goes down, and taking more people on board the already overcrowded raft is gradually bringing its deck even with the water line. You reckon that there must now be four hundred souls aboard. At this rate, the raft is sure to capsize in a matter of seconds.

A few seconds elapse. You can see and feel water lapping at your shoes, but amazingly enough the raft itself is still afloat, and nearly everyone is still busy eating, drinking, or gambling (indeed, the activity around the casino has heated up considerably). You hear someone in the distance shouting about how the raft is about to sink. You rush in the direction of the voice only to see its source being tossed unceremoniously overboard. You decide to keep quiet, but think silently to yourself, "Jeez, this thing *can't* last more than another couple of minutes! What the hell should I do?"

You notice a group of a dozen or so people working to patch and reinforce one corner of the raft. This, at least, is constructive behavior, so you join in. But it's not long before you realize that the only materials available to do the patching with are ones cannibalized from elsewhere on the raft. Even though the people you're working with clearly have the best of intentions and are making some noticeable improvements to the few square feet on which they've worked, there is simply no way they can render the entire vessel "sustainable," given its size, the amount of time required, and the limited availability of basic materials. You think to yourself that there must be some better solution, but can't quite focus on one.

As you stand there fretting, a couple of minutes pass. You realize that every one of your predictions about the fate of the raft has been disconfirmed. You feel useless and silly. You are about to make the only rational deductions — that there must be some mystical power keeping the raft afloat, and that you might as well make the most of the situation and have some barbecue — when a thought comes to you: The "sustainability" crowd has the right idea . . . except that, as they rebuild their corner of the raft, they should make it easily detachable, so that when the boat as a whole sinks they can simply disengage from it and paddle toward shore. But then, what about the hundreds of people who won't be able to fit onto this smaller, reconditioned raftlet?

You notice now that there is a group of rafters grappling with the soldiers who've been shooting holes in canoes. Maybe, if some of the canoes and their indigenous occupants survive, then the scope of the impending tragedy can be reduced. But direct confrontation with the soldiers appears to be a dangerous business, since many of the protesters are being shot or thrown into the water.

You continue working with the sustainability group, since they seem to have the best understanding of the problem and the best chances of survival. At the same time, your sympathies are with the protesters and the fisher families. You hope and pray that this is all some nightmare from which you will soon awaken, or that there is some means of escape — for everyone — that you haven't seen yet.

My goal in writing this book is to provide readers with information that will help them understand the constraints and opportunities of our unique moment in time, so that they can help themselves and the rest of humanity weather the century ahead.

❖ ❖ ❖

The book begins with an overview of oil and natural gas depletion and their likely impacts — a summary and updating of the information in *The Party's Over*. This updated material includes startling information about the current natural gas supply in North America, and the likely geopolitical consequences of attempts by the US to deal with the problem by importing liquefied natural gas from overseas.

In the next four chapters, we explore the four principal options available to industrial societies during the next few decades:

- **Last One Standing — The path of competition for remaining resources.** If the leadership of the US continues with current policies, the next decades will be filled with war, economic crises, and environmental catastrophe. Resource depletion and population pressure are about to catch up with us, and no one is prepared. The political elites, especially in the US, are incapable of dealing with the situation. Their preferred "solution" is simply to comandeer other nations' resources, using military force.
- **Powerdown — The path of cooperation, conservation, and sharing.** The only realistic alternative to resource competition is a strategy that will require tremendous effort and economic sacrifice in order to reduce per-capita resource usage in wealthy countries, develop alternative energy sources, distribute resources more equitably, and humanely but systematically reduce the size of the human population over time. The world's environmental, anti-war, anti-globalization, and human rights organizations are pushing for a mild version of this alternative, but for political reasons they tend to de-emphasize the level of effort required, and to play down the population issue.
- **Waiting for a Magic Elixir — Wishful thinking, false hopes, and denial.** Most of us would like to see still another possibility — a painless transition in which market forces

come to the rescue, making government intervention in the economy unnecessary. I discuss why this rosy hope is extremely unrealistic, and serves primarily as a distraction from the hard work that will be required in order to avert violent competition and catastrophic collapse.

- **Building Lifeboats — The path of community solidarity and preservation.** This fourth and final option begins with the assumption that industrial civilization cannot be salvaged in anything like its present form, and that we are even now living through the early stages of disintegration. If this is so, it makes sense for at least some of us to devote our energies toward preserving the most worthwhile cultural achievements of the past few centuries.

In the final chapter, "Our Choice," I explore how three important groups within global society — the decision-making elites of government, finance, and industry; the opposition to the elites, including the anti-war and anti-globalization movements — the "other superpower"; and ordinary people — are likely to choose among these four options. I suggest that the most fruitful response is likely to be a combination of Powerdown (in its most vigorous form) and Lifeboat Building. This chapter ends with a plea for the conservation of our highest human values and ideals during what is likely to be the most challenging century of all our history.

I believe that attempting to maintain business as usual during the coming decades will merely ensure catastrophic collapse. However, we *can* preserve the best of what we have achieved, while at the same time easing our way as peacefully and equitably as possible back down the steep ramp of increasing scale and complexity our society has been climbing for the past couple of centuries. These are the options we face, and the sooner we acknowledge that this is the case and choose wisely, the better off we and our descendants will be.

CHAPTER ONE

The End of Cheap Energy

*Our prosperity and way of life are sustained
by energy use. [E]nergy security must be a
priority of US trade and foreign policy.*

— National energy policy; *The Cheney Report*,
May 2001

*America faces a major energy supply crisis over the next
two decades. The failure to meet this challenge will
threaten our nation's economic prosperity, compromise
our national security, and literally alter the way
we lead our lives.*

— Secretary of Energy Spencer Abraham, National
Energy Summit, March 19, 2001.

When Mike Bowlin, Chairman of ARCO, said in 1999 that "We've embarked on the beginning of the last days of the age of oil," he was voicing a truth that many others in the petroleum industry knew but dared not utter. Over the past few years, evidence has mounted that global oil production is nearing its historic peak.

Oil has been the cheapest and most convenient energy resource ever discovered by humans. During the past two centuries, people in industrial nations accustomed themselves to a regime in which more fossil-fuel energy was available each year, and the global population grew quickly to take advantage of this energy windfall. Industrial nations also came to rely on an economic system built on the assumption that growth is normal and necessary, and that it can go on forever.

However, that assumption is set to come crashing down. The evidence that oil is about to become less abundant is accumulating quickly.

The oil business started in America in the late nineteenth century, and the US became the most-explored region on the planet — more oil wells have been drilled in the lower-48 states than in all other countries combined. Thus, America's experience with oil will eventually be repeated elsewhere.

Oil *discovery* in the US peaked in the 1930s; US oil *production* peaked roughly forty years later. Since 1970, the US has had to import increasing amounts of oil nearly every year in order to make up for its shortfall from domestic extraction.

Figure 1: The US Discovery and Depletion Profile
The US discovery and depletion profile. (Source: Colin Campbell)

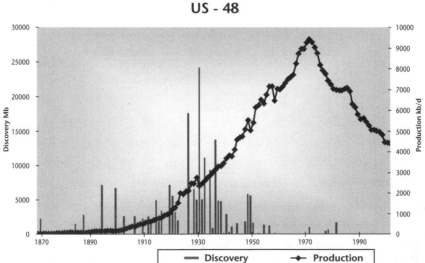

Global discovery of oil peaked in the 1960s. Since production must eventually mirror discovery, global oil production will doubtless peak at some point in the foreseeable future. When, exactly? According to many informed estimates, the peak will occur between 2006 and 2016.

When the global peak in oil production is reached, there will still be plenty of petroleum in the ground — about as much as has been extracted up to the present, or roughly one trillion barrels. But much of the remaining oil will be of lower quality, or more difficult and expensive to access. As a result, every year from then on it will be impossible to pump as much as the year before.

Clearly, we will need to find substitutes for oil. But an analysis of the currently available energy alternatives is not reassuring.

The extraction rate of natural gas will peak globally only a few years after that of liquid petroleum (natural gas production in North America is already falling rapidly, as we will see later in this chapter).

Coal seems relatively abundant until one looks closely: much of what is in the ground is of low quality or will be difficult to extract. The energy profit ratio for coal — the amount of energy it yields minus the amount expended in obtaining the resource — has been falling rapidly over the past decades. If we rely on coal to make up shortfalls from other fossil fuels, extraction rates will peak within decades.[1]

Solar photovoltaics (PV) and wind power are renewable, and production capacity is capable of being greatly expanded (which is not the case with our primary renewable energy source, hydroelectric power). However, we now get only a small fraction of one percent of our national energy budget from them; extremely rapid growth will be necessary if they are to replace even a significant fraction of the energy shortfall from post-peak oil.

Nuclear power is dogged by the unsolved problem of radioactive waste disposal, as well as fears about accidents, terrorism, and diversion of fuels or wastes to weapons programs. To make up for fossil fuel depletion, we would eventually need hundreds of new nuclear plants, and the necessary uranium would run out within just a few decades.

Hydrogen is not an energy source at all, but an energy carrier: it takes more energy to produce a given quantity of hydrogen than the hydrogen itself will yield. Moreover, most commercially produced hydrogen now comes from natural gas — whose global production will peak only a few years after oil begins its historic decline.

Unconventional petroleum resources — so-called "heavy oil," "oil sands," and "shale oil" — are plentiful but extremely costly to extract and process, a fact that no technical innovation is likely to change much (we will discuss hydrogen and unconventional hydrocarbon resources in more detail in Chapter 4).

There are many more possible energy sources for the future — some of them quite promising. But none in sight even comes close to matching the cheapness and convenience of oil during its heyday: after all, nature took millions of years to create petroleum; all we had to do was to extract and burn it. Fossil fuels are the equivalent of a huge inheritance — one that we have spent quickly and not too wisely. Other energy sources will be more analogous to wages: we will have to work for what we get, and our spending will be restricted to immediate income. The hard math of energy resource analysis yields an uncomfortable but unavoidable prospect: even if efforts are intensified now to switch to alternative energy sources, after the global oil peak industrial nations will have less energy available to do useful work — including the manufacturing and transporting of goods, the growing of food, and the heating of homes.

To be sure, we *should be* investing in alternatives and converting our industrial infrastructure to use them. If there is any solution to industrial societies' approaching energy crises, renewables plus conservation will provide it. Yet in order to achieve a smooth transition from non-renewables to renewables, decades will be needed — and we do not have decades before the peak in the extraction rate of oil occurs. Moreover, even in the best case, the transition will require the massive shifting of investment from other sectors of the economy (such as the military) toward energy research and conservation. And the available alternatives will likely be unable to support the *kinds* of transportation, food, and dwelling infrastructure we now have; thus the transition will entail an almost complete redesign of industrial societies.

The likely economic consequences of the coming energy transition will be enormous. All human activities require energy — which physicists define as "the capacity to do work." With less energy available, less work can be done — unless the efficiency of the process of converting energy to work is raised at the same rate as energy availability declines. It will therefore be essential, over the next few decades, for all economic processes to be made more energy-efficient. However, efforts to improve efficiency are subject to diminishing returns, and so eventually a point will be reached where reduced energy availability will translate to reduced economic activity. Given the fact that our national economy is based on the assumption that economic activity must grow perpetually, the result is likely to be a recession with no bottom and no end.

THE PEAK IN PER-CAPITA GLOBAL GRAIN PRODUCTION?
Data for world cereal crops in million tons:
(Source: Food and Agriculture Organization)

Year	Production	Utilization	Reserves
1999	1888.4	1894.4	684.5
2000	1863.2	1915.9	633.4
2001	1906.7	1951	584.2
2002	1832.6	1956.7	466.6
2003	1865.4	1964.1	371.9

Grains constitute 80 to 90 percent of world food supply. In each of the past five years, consumption has outstripped production, and shortfalls have been made up for by the drawing down of reserves. With this year's draw-down, world grain stocks have dropped to the lowest level since the early 1970s, when world prices of wheat and rice doubled as a result. If the recent pace of draw-downs is projected into the future, world grain reserves will be exhausted in the year 2008.

The consequences for global food production will be no less dire. Throughout the 20th century, food production expanded dramatically in country after country, with most of this growth attributable to energy inputs. Without fuel-fed tractors and petroleum-based fertilizers, pesticides, and herbicides, it is doubtful that crop yields can be maintained at current levels.

The oil peak will also impact international relations. Most of the wars of the twentieth century were fought over resources — in many cases, oil. But those wars took place during a period of expanding resource extraction; the coming decades of heightened competition for dwindling energy resources will likely see even more frequent and deadly conflicts. The US — as the world's largest energy consumer, the center of the global industrial empire, and the holder of the most powerful store of weaponry in world history — will play a pivotal role in shaping the geopolitics of the new century. To many observers, it appears that oil interests are already at the heart of the present administration's geopolitical strategy.

There is much that individuals and communities can do to prepare for the energy crunch. Anything that promotes individual self-reliance (gardening, energy conservation, and voluntary simplicity) will help. But the strategy of individualist survivalism will offer only temporary and uncertain refuge during the energy downslope. True individual and family security will come only with community solidarity and interdependence. Living in a community that is weathering the downslope well will enhance personal chances of surviving and prospering far more than will individual efforts at stockpiling tools or growing food.

Meanwhile, nations must adopt radical energy conservation measures, invest in renewable energy research, support sustainable local food systems instead of giant biotech agribusiness, adopt no-growth economic and population policies, and strive for international resource cooperation agreements.

These suggestions describe a fundamental change of direction for industrial societies — from the larger, faster, and more centralized to the smaller, slower, and more locally-based; from competition to cooperation; and from boundless growth to self-limitation.

If such recommendations were taken seriously, they could lead to a world a century from now with fewer people using less energy per capita, all of it from renewable sources, while enjoying a quality of life perhaps enviable by the typical industrial urbanite of today. Human inventiveness could be put to the task, not of making ways to use more resources, but of expanding artistic satisfaction, finding just and convivial social arrangements, and deepening the spiritual experience of being human. Living in smaller communities, people would enjoy having more control over their lives. Traveling less, they would have more of a sense of rootedness, and more of a feeling of being at home in the natural world. Renewable energy sources would provide some conveniences, but not nearly on the scale of fossil-fueled industrialism. This will not, however, be an automatic outcome of the energy decline. Such a happy result can only come about through sustained, coordinated, and strenuous effort.

There are a few hopeful indications that a shift toward sustainability is beginning. But there are also discouraging signs that large political and economic institutions will resist change in that direction. Thus, the most likely trajectory for the energy transition will consist of the collapse of industrial civilization as we know it, probably occurring in stages over a period of several decades. Whether that collapse occurs in a chaotic or controlled way, and whether the generations following the collapse will face bleak or favorable prospects, will depend upon choices we make now.

Recent Confirmations of an Imminent Oil Peak

Confirmation of an imminent oil peak was, in brief, the substance of my previous book, *The Party's Over.* At the time of the book's publication, this was a highly controversial message. Much of it is far less so today.

What has changed? The idea that a geologically-based peak in the rate of global oil extraction is imminent has entered mainstream discussion. The following are a few of the more significant signs that this notion — though still obscure to the average citizen — is not only gaining increasing confirmation from experts, but is becoming a matter of common knowledge among the well-informed.

In an article titled "A Revolutionary Transformation" in *The Lamp,* a quarterly published for ExxonMobil shareholders published in September 2003, exploration division president Jon Thompson reflected on the dramatic changes in exploration technology over the past 40 years and the challenges that lie ahead in finding and producing future supplies of oil and gas. "[W]e estimate that world oil and gas production from existing fields is declining at an average rate of about four to six percent a year," he wrote.

> To meet projected demand in 2015, the industry will have to add about 100 million oil-equivalent barrels a day of new production. That's equal to about 80 percent of today's production level. In other words, by 2015, we will need to find, develop and produce a volume of new oil and gas that is equal to 8 out of every 10 barrels being produced today. In addition, the cost associated with providing this additional oil and gas is expected to be considerably more than what industry is now spending.[2]

Thompson's statements were regarded by many industry insiders as an oblique admission that it will soon be virtually impossible for production levels to keep up with demand.

The reason for Thompson's pessimism could be discerned in facts elucidated in an article by Richard C. Duncan of the Institute on Energy and Man in Seattle, titled "Three World Oil Forecasts Predict Peak Oil Production," published in the May 26, 2003 issue of *Oil and Gas Journal.* Duncan noted that "Forecasts of the imminent depletion of oil are as old as the industry itself, and that has not changed. What has changed is the growing amount of historical oil data now available to test forecasts."[3] Of the 44 significant oil-producing nations, at least 24 are clearly past their peak of production, according to Duncan. Thus, the discussion about an approaching global oil production peak is ever less about prognostication, and more about simple observation and the recording of history as it happens.

Article after article sounded a similar note. In a piece titled "Critical Paths to the Post-Petroleum Age," Russell A. Brown of Argonne National Laboratory concluded:

> World petroleum production will begin to decline during the next decade. The majority of the petroleum-producing nations have already passed their production peaks. . . . The United States has compensated for its production decline by importing oil. The planet does not have that option. . . . The United States and the world face an energy problem that goes far beyond the need for developing new technologies or building more power plants. . . . Preparation for both these changes and their effects must begin immediately.[4]

Figure 2: Global Oil Depletion Scenario

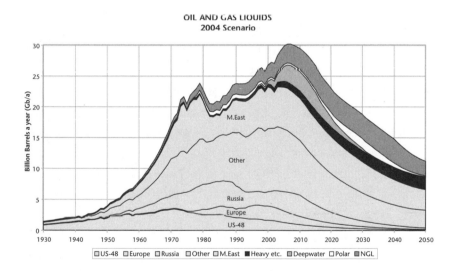

The Association for the Study of Peak Oil (ASPO) publishes a frequently updated chart of the global oil depletion scenario, history and forecast. The forecast currently shows a peak for all petroleum liquids around 2007. (www.peakoil.net)

An important paper by Werner Zittel and Jörg Schindler (who have served as scientific advisers to the German parliament) titled "Future World Oil Supply" appeared first in July 2002, but came under increasing discussion in the English-speaking world during 2003. Toward the end of their paper, Zittel and Schindler summarized their main facts, theses, and conclusions as follows:

- The peak of oil discoveries was reached in the 1960s. . . .
- This peak in discoveries has to be followed by a peak in production, since we can only produce what has been found before.
- The production peak of individual fields is a historical fact, [and] almost all large oil fields have already passed their production maximum and are in decline.
- The aggregation of the production profiles of individual fields (with their individual peaks) sums up to a production peak of individual oil regions. Historically, peak production was reached in Austria in 1955, in Germany in 1968, in the USA in 1971, in Indonesia in 1977. Recent regions joining the club of countries with declining production rates are Gabon (1997), UK (1999), Australia (2000), Oman (2000), and Norway (2001).
- The aggregate decline of mature regions is getting steeper with every new "member of the club." In order to keep overall production just flat, ever fewer regions have to increase their production.
- This pattern [has been observed for] more than thirty years. . . . It is very likely that the peak of world oil production will be reached [before] 2010 at the latest.[5]

On November 28, 2003, at a conference on energy and the environment organized by the Royal Society of Canada, University of British Columbia professor of human ecology William Rees, widely known for devising the "ecological footprint" method of measuring environmental impact, forecast that world combined conventional and non-conventional oil and gas liquids production will peak before 2017. This is, in fact, a fairly optimistic date when compared to the predictions of oil industry cassandras like Colin Campbell and Kenneth Deffeyes, who expect the peak to occur within the next few years. Nevertheless, Rees stated that social and political shock waves will be felt when the peak occurs, because alternative sources of energy will be unable to deliver the quality and quantity of energy to which industrial societies have become accustomed.[6]

In mid-2003, both the US Energy Information Agency (EIA) and the International Energy Agency (IEA) announced that world excess oil production capacity (oil that can potentially be extracted over and above immediate demand) was then at its lowest point in 30 years — less than one million barrels per day.[7] Excess capacity was lower then even than in 1991, when Kuwaiti and Iraqi production were off-stream because of the Gulf War. Nearly all of the existing spare production capacity exists either in Russia or in Arab OPEC countries. During the winter of 2003–2004, US supplies tightened to their lowest levels since 1975, due to increased demand in the face of tight OPEC production quotas. In January 2004, the US had a mere 13 days' worth of oil supply in reserve, and refineries were running at close to 100 percent of capacity.[8]

This problem appeared to be the result of long-term trends rather than short-term market vagaries. A report commissioned by vice president Dick Cheney from the US Council on Foreign Relations and the Baker Institute for Public Policy, titled "Strategic Energy Policy Challenges for the 21st Century," and released in April 2001, had stated:

> Perhaps the most significant difference between now and a decade ago is the extraordinarily rapid erosion of spare capacities at critical segments of energy chains. Today, shortfalls appear to be endemic. Among the most extraordinary of these losses of spare capacity is in the oil arena.[9]

The report noted that in 1985, OPEC spare production capacity stood at 25 percent of total global demand; in 1990, eight percent;

in 2001, just two. The report called this shortfall a matter of strategic significance, as interruptions from terrorism or other political factors could cripple the American economy: "The world is currently precariously close to utilizing all of its available global oil production capacity, raising the chances of an oil supply crisis with more substantial consequences than seen in three decades."[10]

However, the picture may be even bleaker than the Baker policy paper suggested, as some experts now believe that OPEC excess capacity has been overestimated. In recent reports, the US Department of Energy has revised downward some of its estimates of excess capacity in Kuwait and Indonesia. And oil analyst Matthew Simmons is currently at work on a book in which he calls into question the actual production capabilities of Saudi Arabia, the nation with the world's foremost reserves and the "swing producer" that for decades has had the power to set global oil prices. Simmons has concluded, after a review of roughly 150 technical papers written since 1962 by geologists and engineers at Saudi Aramco and its predecessor, Aramco, that Saudi production may be within years of peaking. Saudi oil structures are "heterogeneous," with complex underground fractures that can impede recovery. Since the 1970s, the Saudis have used a recovery technique known as "water injection," in which heavy, salty water is pumped into the reservoirs to push oil to the surface. Simmons notes that the Saudis are currently injecting about seven million barrels a day of seawater. "Water injection gives the appearance of eternal youth," according to Simmons. "That's why the Saudi fields look so robust." However, injection can damage wells and could prevent the recovery of predicted quantities. If Saudi Arabia — the country on which the rest of the world relies for excess capacity — is itself close to a peak in production, then a global oil peak could be imminent.[11]

On October 2, 2003, the *Independent* of London reported on research at the University of Uppsala in Sweden forecasting a "production crunch" for world oil and gas supplies sometime between 2010 and 2020:

While forecasters have always known that such a date lies ahead, they have previously put it around 2050, and estimated that there would be time to shift energy use over to renewables and other non-fossil sources. But Kjell Aleklett, one of a team of geologists that prepared the report, said earlier estimates that the world's entire reserve amounts to 18,000 billion barrels of oil and gas — of which about 1,000 billion has been used up so far — were "completely unrealistic." He, Anders Sivertsson and Colin Campbell told *New Scientist* magazine that less than 3,500 billion barrels of oil and gas remained in total. . . . Present annual oil consumption is about 25 billion barrels, and shows no signs of slowing. That would suggest a "production crunch" — where consumption grows to meet the maximum output — within the next couple of decades.[12]

In its November 20, 2003 issue, the prestigious British science journal *Nature* featured an article by a group of environmental scientists led by Charles Hall of the State University of New York at Syracuse, titled "Hydrocarbons and the Evolution of Human Culture." That article concluded:

The world is not about to run out of hydrocarbons, and perhaps it is not going to run out of oil from unconventional sources any time soon. What will be difficult to obtain is cheap petroleum, because what is left is an enormous amount of low-grade hydrocarbons, which are likely to be much more expensive financially, energetically, politically and especially environmentally.[13]

Former UK environment minister Michael Meacher put the matter more starkly in an article, "Plan Now for a World Without Oil," in the January 5, 2004 edition of the *Financial Times:*

> The world faces a stark choice. It can continue down the existing path of rising oil consumption, trying to pre-empt available remaining oil supplies, if necessary by military force, but without avoiding a steady exhaustion of global capacity. Or it could switch to renewable sources of energy, much more stringent standards of energy efficiency, and a steady reduction in oil use. The latter course would involve huge new investment in energy generation and transportation technologies.

According to an analysis of existing and planned major oil-recovery projects published in the February, 2004 edition of *Petroleum Review*, global oil supplies may have difficulty meeting growing demand after 2007. While production from many new off-shore wells will hit the market over the next three years, the *Oil Field Mega Projects 2004* report notes, the volumes produced are likely to fall off quickly thereafter. "There are not enough large-scale projects in the development pipeline right now to offset declining production in mature areas and meet global demand growth beyond 2007," says Chris Skrebowski, author of the report and editor of *Petroleum Review*. "Ever-growing demand for oil means there is a ready market for additional supplies so substantial new discoveries tend to go into development in a very limited time," Skrebowski notes. "But between a quarter and a third of the world's oil production is already in decline and it appears that giant new discoveries to replace lost capacity are becoming very scarce."[14]

The report also documents that the rate of discoveries of major new oil fields has fallen dramatically in recent years: There were 13 discoveries of over 500 million barrels in 2000, six in 2001 and just two in 2002. For 2003, not a single new discovery over 500 million barrels was reported.

This falling discovery trend was confirmed by another recent report, this one by energy consultant Wood Mackenzie. This latter report points out that the ten largest energy companies in 2001 and

2002 lost money on exploration; that is, the oil they found was not worth the amount invested. The average size of the new fields is 50 million barrels — which must be considered in context of the fact that the world uses roughly 75 million barrels per day. The oil companies are currently finding a total of about 20 million barrels per day.[15]

Figure 3: New Commercial Discoveries

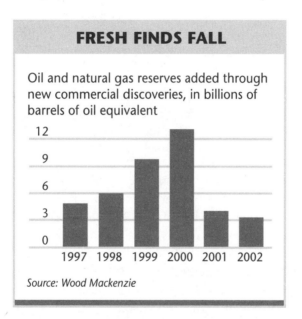

Source: Wood Mackenzie

At this writing, petroleum economist Andrew McKillop is at work on a new book, *The Final Energy Crisis;* his introduction warns:

> If we shift the clock forward to 2035 we can maybe better understand our predicament. By 2035 oil production will likely be 75 percent down on the coming peak, and gas production about 60 percent down. Entire "new oil provinces" like the North Sea will have disappeared at least 10 years before, not even remaining as small, residual production zones. By 2035, US domestic oil and gas production will be practically non-existent. By 2035, the maximum rate of oil production,

even in today's large producer countries like Saudi Arabia and Russia, will have declined significantly. For Russia its output will only be a fraction of current production. Well before 2035, many current oil exporters with large populations, or whose domestic oil demand is growing fast, and whose production capacity is near or beyond peak, will be simply forced to curtail all export of oil. For countries such as Iran, Indonesia, Venezuela, and Nigeria such decisions, with inevitable and unstoppable upward oil price impacts, could come in just the next 10 years.[16]

Oil companies themselves are increasingly being forced to admit that a supply crisis is on the horizon, as was made apparent in an announcement by Shell earlier this year, reported by Bloomberg:

> Royal Dutch/Shell Group, Europe's second-largest oil company, slashed its estimate of proved oil and gas reserves by a fifth and for a third year in a row failed to find as much oil as it pumped. The shares sank 7.5 percent. The revision means Shell's proved reserves at the end of 2002 were about 16 billion barrels, rather than the 20 billion stated earlier. A 3.9 billion-barrel difference still has "scope for recovery" and may ultimately be produced, said spokesman Andy Corrigan. London-based Shell estimated that it replaced 70 percent to 90 percent of its output in 2003, excluding acquisitions. Shell's statement, its second unexpected disclosure in two weeks, comes amid investor concern about growth at the company's exploration and production division, its most profitable unit. In October, the company said it would miss its production target for 2003.[17]

Finally, production from Russia — currently the world's second foremost oil exporter — will cease growth in 2007, according to LUKoil vice president Leonid Fedun. Currently Russia exports oil to Europe and Asia, and recent hikes in Russian production have served to offset declines from other post-peak nations such as Venezuela and Iran. When Russian production begins its decline, Saudi Arabia will be virtually the only significant producer capable of making up for shortfalls in global supply (see Simmons excerpts, page 28).[18]

To be sure, the cornucopian view of a world forever awash in cheap oil still prevails in some quarters. In its July 14, 2003 edition, *Oil & Gas Journal* included an article titled "The New Pessimism about Petroleum Resources: Debunking the Hubbert Model (and Hubbert Modelers)," by oil economist Michael C. Lynch, which put forward the well-worn notion that "reserve growth" will cancel the effects of depletion for at least the next three decades. (For a discussion on this point, see *The Party's Over*, pages 112–117.)

The April 22, 2003 edition of the *San Francisco Chronicle* carried an op-ed piece by Daniel Yergin (chair of Cambridge Energy Research Associates and author of *The Prize: The Epic Quest for Oil, Money, and Power*), suggesting that new sources in the Persian Gulf, West Africa, Canada, and elsewhere, plus new technology and reserve growth, will satisfy global oil demand as it expands from the current 77 million barrels per day to over 90 million barrels per day by 2020. Yergin concluded: "The point here is that world oil supplies are not some finite constant sum. Rather, the picture is dynamic and changing. The reserve picture will continue to shift."

And the cover of the October 25, 2003 edition of *The Economist* featured a photo of rusting gasoline pumps with a bold title, "The end of the Oil Age." However, the accompanying article turned out to be not about petroleum depletion, but the promise of alternative energy sources. The piece commenced with a hackneyed quote from Sheikh Zaki Yamani, former oil minister of Saudi Arabia: "The Stone Age did not end for lack of stone, and the Oil Age will end long before the world runs out of oil."

But while the oil optimists appeared confident, their forecasts, when examined closely, predicted only that the global peak will come a few years later than is forecast by the pessimists — perhaps by 2030 or 2035, instead of the pessimists' 2004 to 2016 range.

Even if we accept the optimists' view of future supply, industrial societies have a huge problem on their hands. The Age of Oil is indeed about to come to an end, by *everyone's* estimates.

In short, a bit of information that was little-heard and controversial at the beginning of 2003 seems to have been confirmed, and has gotten out to a much larger audience. However, its true significance has yet to sink in.

The Petroleum Plateau — and Beyond

The realization that the industrial world is approaching the peak in available net energy to fuel the global economy comes as a powerful shock to one's belief system.[19] It literally changes everything. And once one has a clear mental picture of the grand bell-shaped curve of energy usage in the industrial era, the fine detail within that curve becomes a matter of more than passing interest. A bump on the curve may mean a war, a recession, or a significant change of government policy with immense implications for the lives of millions of people.

The terms "oil production peak" and "peak oil" imply a sharp demarcation. One naturally envisions a needle-like moment in time: before the fateful day, oil production wafts ever upward; then, suddenly, the trend reverses. In a flash, economies crumble and our energy-dependent way of life is on its way to an inevitable, crashing end.

This, of course, is an oversimplification. The graph of global oil extraction is not taking the form of the classic bell-shaped Hubbert curve, with a slender, rounded peak (for a discussion of M. King Hubbert and an explanation of the Hubbert curve, see *The Party's Over,* pp. 88 – 92); instead, it appears more like bumpy mesa — a flat-topped mountain — covered with rubble. A steep runup in extraction, lasting until the early 1970s, was followed by an uneven plateau and will no doubt be followed by a similarly steep decline.

Figure 4

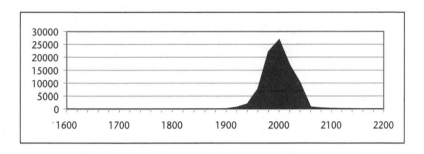

Oil production from deep historical perspective, in millions of barrels per year. From a distance, it looks like a sharp peak.

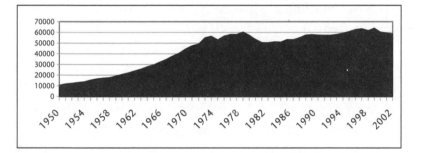

Conventional oil production from a closer perspective: the plateau becomes clearly visible — 1973 to present. In thousands of barrels per day.

Why the plateau? Oil production is constrained by economic conditions (in an economic downturn, demand for oil falls off), as well as by political events such as wars and revolutions. In addition, the shape of the production curve is modified by the increasing availability of unconventional petroleum sources (including heavy oil, natural gas plant liquids, and tar sands), as well as new extraction technologies. The combined effect of all of these factors is to cushion the peak and lengthen the decline curve.

Political-economic events during the 1970s caused a preliminary global oil peak. The following worldwide recession suppressed demand for energy, while efficiency measures (increasing the insulation of homes and office buildings, lowering highway speed limits, etc.) stretched the benefits from temporarily expensive fuels. Oil production and consumption took a brief dive after the 1973 OPEC oil embargo (falling from a peak of 56 million barrels per day in 1974), then began to recover — though on average the growth rate was lower than in previous years. Production reached a new peak of 60 million barrels per day in 1979. Then, following the 1979 Iranian revolution, production and consumption plummeted again and did not begin to increase until 1984; production did not again match its 1979 levels until 1996. In the four years following that, production of conventional oil inched higher still, to a new peak of nearly 64 million barrels per day in 2000 (the figure for total petroleum liquids, including non-conventional sources, by then surpassed 76 million barrels per day).

This historical period — in which conventional oil production has been, when averaged, relatively flat — will probably eventually be seen as the first stage in an energy plateau encompassing the period from 1973 to perhaps 2015 — nearly a half a century. During this plateau period, production and consumption of conventional oil will be seen to have crested and bottomed several times between the extremes of 65 million barrels per day and 50 million barrels per day.

We are living toward the end of this historic energy plateau right now. The plateau began because of political and economic events. Soon, geological factors will begin to constrain conventional oil extraction. Already, natural gas depletion has begun to wreak economic havoc in North America, as we will discuss in more detail below. These constraints will intensify and gradually gain hold over the world energy supply, so that by 2016 at the very latest, and possibly within just two or three years, global energy availability will be on an inexorable downward trend somewhat mirroring the historic upswing of the early 20th century.

The fact that we have arrived at an energy plateau means that two centuries of energy growth are at an end; a century of decline is about to begin. We are in a place betwixt and between, neither this nor that. This is a unique period that brings unique opportunities

and challenges; it is a temporal terrain whose navigation will determine whether our path down the energy curve is quick and disastrous, or measured and deliberate.

Surveying the Plateau

Before exploring those opportunities and challenges, we should first
reconnoiter the energy situation as it has developed so far during the
plateau period.

For readers who are interested in studying the data for themselves, excellent sources are readily available. I recommend the website of the Energy Information Administration (EIA), a division of
the US Department of Energy, which offers dozens of free down-
loadable databases.[20] The Central Intelligence Agency web site also
offers a treasure trove of statistical demographic data for the asking.[21] The picture that emerges from such a study clearly confirms
the fact of the plateau, but contains many layers of complex detail.

Since economic activity requires work, and since energy is the
capacity to perform work, energy is therefore necessary for economic growth. Thus it come as no surprise that the oil plateau represents
a period of slower economic growth as compared with the preceding decades of increasing energy abundance. Between 1950 and
1973, economic growth ranged between 2.1 percent for the US and
7.4 percent for Japan, per annum, for the G7 countries; whereas
since 1973 economic growth has averaged 0.6 percent for the US
and 2.6 percent for Japan. For mainstream economists, the "post-
1973 productivity slowdown" is, in the words of UC Berkeley economist J. Bradford deLong, "a mystery." But it is a mystery explained
almost instantly when one beholds a graph of total or per-capita
energy usage from 1900 to the present.

But this is still not the whole picture. From 1900 to 1973, standards of living (as measured by GDP per capita) rose across the
board, in rich and poor countries alike — though at differing rates
and with intermittent peaks and valleys. During the plateau period
(1973 to present), living standards in other industrialized countries
(Europe, Japan) largely caught up with those in the US. But during

this same period, economic inequality between the richest countries on one hand, and the poorest on the other, and between high-income and low-income groups within the populations of some important countries (such as the US), has increased markedly.

Let us look at this disparity in energy terms. While oil is in many respects our most important energy resource, it is not the only one. During the past thirty years, total global energy use (from sources including coal, natural gas, nuclear, and hydro power) has grown, though — as mentioned earlier — at a rate slower than in the period prior to 1973. Currently, there is a dramatic disparity in per-capita energy use between the more- and less-industrialized nations. For example, in 1997, Americans used energy at a rate equivalent to 8,076 kilograms of oil per capita, versus 479 kilograms for India. It is interesting to note that the figures for Japan

THE DEPLETION-LED DECLINE OF THE US

Many people tend to assume that the social and economic effects of oil depletion will be felt sometime in the future, if at all. However, an examination of recent history shows that Americans have already paid a high price as a result of the peaking and decline of their domestic petroleum extraction.

In the early 20th century, the US was the world's foremost oil-producing and oil-exporting nation, as well as being the world's top oil consumer. The US quickly became the most-explored region of the planet for petroleum. Oil discovery peaked in the 1930s with tremendous finds in Texas, but declined rapidly afterward despite ongoing intensive exploration.

Oil helped make the US the world's economic and military giant: most of the petroleum used by the allies to win the World Wars came from American wells, and after 1945 the nation was in position to become the world's foremost lender, helping to rehabilitate Europe and Japan.

American oil production peaked in 1970–71. Already the US was importing cheaper oil from abroad, but now it was clear that and the European countries are about half those for the US (4,084 for Japan, 2,839 for Italy). Only Canada, among the industrial nations (at 7,930), has a per-capita appetite for energy approaching that of the US. Through greater efficiency, the Europeans and Japanese are able to achieve a standard of living comparable to that of North Americans.

Adding population growth to the equation overlays still another helpful level of detail. Since 1973, the world's population has grown from fewer than 4 billion to over 6.4 billion, and most of that growth has taken place in the poorer countries, which are of course the ones that use less energy on a per-capita basis. Recall that oil production stood at 56 million barrels per day in 1974, and that today, production of conventional oil is in the vicinity of 70 mb/d. Clearly population growth has far outstripped growth in production of conventional oil.

an ever-greater percentage of its energy needs would have to be filled by oil purchased elsewhere. The 1973 Arab oil embargo drove home the geopolitical consequences of increasing American petro-dependency. With the fall of the Shah of Iran in 1979, president Jimmy Carter formalized what would become known as the Carter Doctrine, which stated that America would use its military to maintain access to the oil reserves of the Middle East.

Since its 1970 oil peak, the US has suffered a slow but inexorable economic decline. Formerly the world's foremost creditor nation, it has become by far the world's foremost debtor nation. Once the producer of 60 percent of the world's manufactured products, the US now imports automobiles, consumer electronics, machine tools, and clothing: meanwhile manufacturing jobs continue to flee across its borders.

Of course, history is complex, and it would be a mistake to ascribe all of America's economic and geopolitical woes to oil depletion. However, it is clear that recent US history is marked by increasing energy dependency and decreasing solvency. The economic and geopolitical impacts of oil depletion are not hypothetical; they are a matter of historical record.

THE CIA'S INTEREST IN PEAK OIL

A recently declassified CIA document casts new light on some of the most significant geopolitical events of the past quarter century. This document, an Intelligence Memorandum titled "The Impending Soviet Oil Crisis (ER 77-10147)," was issued in March 1977 by the Office of Economic Research and classified "Secret" until its public release in January 2001 in response to a Freedom of Information Act (FOIA) request. (To access the document, go to <www.foia.cia.gov>. In the document search field, type <er 77-10147>.)

The Memorandum predicts an impending peak in Soviet oil production "not later than the early 1980s" (the actual peak occurred in 1987 at 12.6 million barrels per day, following a preliminary peak in 1983 of 12.5 millions of barrels per day). "During the next decade," the unnamed authors of the document conclude, "the USSR may well find itself not only unable to supply oil to Eastern Europe and the West on the present scale, but also having to compete for OPEC oil for its own use." The Memorandum predicts that the oil peak will have important economic impacts: "When oil production stops growing, and perhaps even before, profound repercussions will be felt on the domestic economy of the USSR and on its international economic relations."

The significance of this document requires some unpacking. First, we must understand the historical context in which it appeared. Oil production in the US had peaked in 1970, just a few years earlier. This was arguably the most important economic event of the past half-century: until then America was the world's foremost oil producer; for much of the 20th century it was also the world's foremost oil exporter. America's oil made it the world's richest and most powerful nation. Meanwhile, throughout most of this same period, the USSR remained the world's second foremost oil-producing nation.

The American oil peak signaled the end of an era: from that point on, the US would become increasingly dependent on imports

— and this dependence would entail serious costs, as became apparent with the Arab OPEC oil embargo of 1973, which sent the US economy into a tailspin. Clearly, CIA analysts in 1977 understood the importance of the American oil peak and believed that a peak of petroleum production in the USSR would have similar or even graver consequences for that nation.

This much is clear and undisputable. Less clear is what was done with the information. Soon after assuming office in 1981, the Reagan Administration abandoned the established policy of pursuing détente with the Soviet Union, and instead instituted a massive arms buildup; it also fomented proxy wars in areas of Soviet influence, while denying the Soviets desperately needed oil equipment and technology. Then, in the mid-1980s, Washington persuaded Saudi Arabia to flood the world market with cheap oil. Throughout the last decade of its existence, the USSR pumped and sold its oil at the maximum possible rate in order to earn foreign exchange income with which to keep up in the arms race and continue its war in Afghanistan. Yet with markets awash in cheap Saudi oil, the Soviets were earning less, even as they pumped more. Two years after Soviet oil production peaked, the economy of the USSR crumbled and its government collapsed.

It seems likely that the Reagan administration based its Cold War strategy on the CIA study, in the expectation that a Soviet Union economically weakened by oil depletion would collapse if pushed hard on other fronts.

The 1977 CIA document shows clear and detailed awareness of oil issues, including depletion, extraction technologies, pipelines, areas of likely new discovery, the quality of existing reserves, and the dynamics of the global oil market. The CIA has obviously been studying oil very carefully for some time and must therefore understand the issue of global oil peak. This begs the questions: Does the Agency have a strategy for dealing with this impending mega-event? Or is the Agency's job merely to provide information, and allow the current administration to formulate policy?

Indeed, global *per-capita* consumption of oil has shrunk, on average, by over one percent per year since 1979. But again, that average figure hides the increasing level of energy inequity, which only becomes apparent when one examines the figures nation-by-nation. Between 1991 and 2000, total energy use increased in the US by 17.3 percent, but in the rest of the world by only 9.9 percent. During this same decade global population grew by nearly 800 million, or roughly 15 percent, while population in the US grew by only 10 percent. Thus people in the US were *increasing* their energy use per capita, while those in the rest of the world were, on average, *decreasing* theirs noticeably. China is the main less-industrialized country that is significantly growing its per-capita energy use.

Still another important level of detail concerns *non-conventional* oil sources — heavy oil, polar oil, deepwater oil, tar sands, and natural gas liquids — which are typically more expensive to produce than is conventional oil. In the early 1970s, these sources made up an insignificant part of the total global oil market, but today they account for more than 10 percent of total oil produced. The EIA gives current oil production at about 83 million barrels per day, of which nearly 10 million barrels per day is from non-conventional sources. A consumption curve that takes these sources into account shows oil production growing more steeply from 1984 on, as compared to a graph of conventional oil only.

Analysis of these statistics suggests that the plateau period that began in the early 1970s is divisible into sectors.

First, there are *temporal sectors,* or stages.

- The plateau begins with the peak in oil production in 1970–71 in the US — the country where the oil industry started, and the most thoroughly explored and exploited oil-producing province in the world.
- The first stage of the plateau (1970–1984) was characterized by limits to energy growth issuing mostly from political events, and by the increasing reliance by the US upon oil imports. Efforts toward increased energy conservation commenced.

- The second stage (1984–1990) was a time of intensified Cold War and the fraying of the Soviet empire (see sidebar on page 41). Oil prices fell, and some efforts toward energy conservation were abandoned. The world economy began a partial recovery from the oil shocks of the 1970s, though at a lower overall rate of growth.
- The third stage (1990–2000) corresponds with the era of economic globalization, in which the industrial system was restructured to shift production to areas with lower labor cost, and to guarantee industrialized nations' access to resources elsewhere through global trade agreements. Total energy use continued to grow, primarily in the US and in industrialized or industrializing East Asian countries, still in most cases at a slower rate than the pre-1973 years.

Figure 5

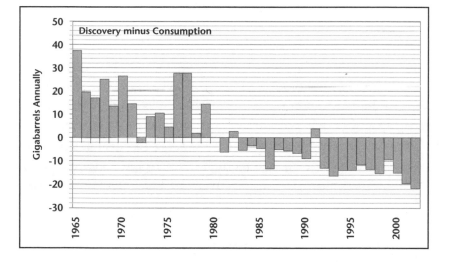

Until well into the 1970s, new global oil discoveries were more than sufficient to offset production each year. Since 1981, the amount of new oil discovered each year has been less than the amount extracted and used.

- The fourth stage (2000–present) represents a period of increasing economic constraints due partly to the gradual appearance of actual resource limits (the peak in production of North Sea oil and the peaking of natural gas production in North America); to political and geopolitical events (the ascendancy of the neoconservatives in the US; 9/11 and its aftermath; the Afghanistan and Iraq invasions); and to diminishing economic returns from the strategy of corporate globalization. This period is also characterized by increasing reliance on more expensive non-conventional petroleum sources
- The fifth stage will begin when it is clear that geological limits are constraining economic activity and will continue to do so despite any and all efforts. The first sign of stage five is probably the natural gas shortages in North America now commencing.

Then, on a separate axis, one can visualize four *economic sectors* within the plateau:

- The US and Canada, with per-capita rates of energy usage roughly twice those of other industrialized nations (8,076 and 7,930 kilograms of oil-equivalent energy used per capita per year in 1997, respectively).
- Europe and Japan (range: Spain, 2,729 to Finland, 6,435).
- The less-industrialized world, with per-capita rates of energy use less than one-quarter to about one-half those of most European countries (range: Bangladesh, 197 to Brazil, 1,051).
- OPEC nations, whose per-capita energy use ranges between those of sectors two and three (Indonesia, 693 to Kuwait, 8,936 — the latter consumption figure surpassing that of the US). This sector itself thus needs to be subdivided into "rich OPEC" (Kuwait and Saudi Arabia) and "poor OPEC" (Indonesia, Nigeria, Iran, Iraq, Algeria, and Venezuela).

History might have been different. If the oil crises of the 1970s had not occurred, the global use of oil might have conformed more closely to the classic Hubbert bell curve; the peak of the curve for oil extraction would have come and gone in the 1990s, and we might now be in the midst of social and economic chaos.

The fact that we are in a plateau period that began nearly three decades ago and that may continue, in some form, for another decade or so means that we may have some room for maneuvering. However, there is no guarantee that we will make constructive use of this borrowed time. Just as humans became accustomed to the age of rapid energy growth (1800–1973) and assumed that it would last forever, many people have become accustomed to life on the plateau and assume that it, too, will persist indefinitely. Humans seem genetically hardwired to react to problems on only a relatively immediate basis.[22] Problems that take years or decades to manifest require us to exercise faculties of analysis and response that are poorly developed in most citizens, and indeed in most of our social and economic institutions and their managers.

Nevertheless the plateau period is a time of fateful choice. It is possible — likely, in fact — that we will collectively fail to recognize the nature of our dilemma, and will hence suffer the consequences. However, it is theoretically possible for us to foresee those consequences and plan for a difficult but survivable transition to a lower-energy regime, as we will see in Chapter 3.

The Natural Gas Quandary

Now add to the global oil predicament the natural gas crisis in North America.

Natural gas, which accounts for 24 percent of the total energy used in the US, is increasingly the fuel of choice for home heating, industrial processes (including plastics, chemical, and fertilizer manufacturing), and electrical power generation. More than half of American homes already heat with gas, and for new homes the proportion is higher. Over $100 billion in new gas-fired electrical generation capacity has been ordered or built in the past five years.

Natural gas's growing popularity is largely due to the fact that it is less polluting than either coal or oil: with fewer carbon atoms in its molecular chains, it produces fewer pollutants — including carbon dioxide — when burned. Natural gas has also been plentiful and inexpensive — until recently.

Because it is invisible, natural gas is easy to take for granted. Now, of course, many people are aware that the US faces a gas supply crisis. Prices have skyrocketed, from around $2 per thousand cubic feet (mcf) before the autumn of 2000, to $8 early this year (on January 14, 2004, the New York Gate price hit $47.50). Moreover, widespread reliance on gas for electrical power generation means that blackouts resulting from gas shortages are becoming increasingly likely. Nevertheless, while nearly everyone is upset about the shortages and high prices, it is surprising how seldom one hears or reads the word that most clearly sums up the cause of the dilemma — *depletion*.

The nub of the issue is that North America has passed its peak in natural gas production. US production peaked in 1971, but the country managed to maintain a fairly flat production curve until the end of the 1990s by steeply increasing investment in exploration and recovery. By 2002, the US was importing 15 percent of its gas from Canada; meanwhile, Mexico — which had been *exporting* gas north of the border — had begun *importing* gas from the US. In 2003, it became clear that Canada's production was also in decline.

Demand for natural gas follows a fairly predictable seasonal cycle. During the summer, marginal demand depends largely on the peaking demand for electricity for air conditioning (many gas-fired "peaking" generating plants only come on line when needed on particularly hot days). However, gas demand is usually even higher during the winter, when homes must be heated. Thus, during the warmer months, managers of the continental distribution system inject gas into underground storage caverns; during the winter, the stored gas is withdrawn. All year long, however, weather is crucial; pressure must be maintained in thousands of miles of gas pipelines, because if the pressure drops too much, the entire system goes down.

The symptoms of an imminent shortage began in the winter of 2000, when a dramatic gas price spike (from $2/mcf to over $10) helped torpedo the longest economic boom in modern US history. By the winter of 2002–2003, gas in underground storage was at historically low levels, prices were at or near historic highs, and industry officials were mumbling about facing difficulties in replenishing reserves before the next winter's draw-down began.

An article in the February 24, 2003 issue of *Oil & Gas Journal* noted:

> The US appears on the verge of another major natural gas supply shortage, Raymond James & Associates Inc. said upon receiving full results from a fourth quarter 2002 US natural gas production survey of 37 companies. "Indications are that US natural gas production has declined by 2.7 percent sequentially and 6.4 percent year-over-year," said RJA analyst Marshall Adkins. Previously, based upon results from 29 companies, RJA had forecast a 0.6 percent decline by quarter sequentially and a 4.6 percent decline on a [year-on-year] basis.

Meanwhile, industry news from north of the US-Canadian border was typified by a Reuters story by Jeffrey Jones, dated March 3, 2003:

> Nova Scotia's dream of soon being a major supplier of offshore gas could be in jeopardy unless oil companies — which have sunk millions of dollars into unsuccessful wells — make some big finds in the next two or three years, a senior industry official said on Monday . . . . Development of Nova Scotia's offshore gas fields has been hit by a string of setbacks, including several expensive dry holes and EnCana Corp.'s (ECA.TO) decision last month to put the brakes on development of its Can$1.1 billion (US$740 million) Deep Panuke project.

As gas prices rose, whole industries shut down. Producers of nitrogen fertilizer were among the first to be affected, followed by the chemical industry. By early 2003, a quarter of the US fertilizer factories had been shut down permanently, and another quarter were idled until prices settled back. According to a March 10 article in *Chemical & Engineering News*, titled "Feedstock Prices Soar, Firms Reel: Chemical industry combats the rising costs of natural gas and oil:"

> The chemical industry is reeling from last month's record run-up in natural gas prices. Chemical makers have throttled back output and are trying to pass costs along to customers. Wall Street and industry groups, meanwhile, are warning of deteriorating business conditions.

Gas prices fell somewhat during the summer of 2003, but still remained at over twice the previous year's levels. North Americans scraped through that unusually mild season without obvious problems, but by early 2004, concerns were being raised about the remaining winter months, and the seasons that would follow. Clearly, the nation cannot count on perpetually mild winters and summers. The situation has grown so delicate that a single month of unusually hot or cold weather is capable of triggering either a severe gas shortage or electrical blackouts.

Interruptions in electrical service have already become more common. The great August 14 blackout of 2003 affected over 50 million homes and businesses in the US and Canada. In recent years, growth in generation capacity has not been matched by reinforcement of the transmission infrastructure, and so the system has become increasingly unstable. (It is worth noting in passing that other countries are also facing problems with inadequate electrical generating capacity or the fragility of transmission systems: persistent power shortages in southern China are such that domestic customers spend one day out of four without power, and the year 2003 saw major blackouts not just in the US but in Chile, the Czech Republic, London, Italy, Sweden, Denmark, Buenos Aires, and Malaysia.)

Andrew Weissman, publisher of *Energy Business Watch* and chairman of Energy Ventures Group, summarized the perils of the North American gas situation in an interview with Bill Powers of *Canadian Energy Viewpoint* in January 4, 2004:

> Between now and 2015, the cumulative [natural gas] deficit [will be] on the order of 50 Tcf [trillion cubic feet]. This is comparable to 50 percent of total US energy consumption in every sector, excluding only mobile sources, in any one year. I believe that if the public better understood the dimensions of this shortfall there would be — and in fact should be — an outburst of concern. Modern economies cannot function without adequate energy supplies and feedstock for key manufacturing processing. From the evidence now available, it is apparent that over the remainder of this decade, we are likely to run desperately short of supplies of natural gas . . . which had been expected to be the fuel experiencing the most growth and for which, in the short to mid-term, for the most part, no substitutes are available.[23]

Clearly, the US and Canada face a problem of mammoth proportions. What are the options?

One would be simply to tell the people of these nations the truth — that natural gas supplies are in decline and will never recover; to conserve what remains of this important resource; and to fund a transition to renewable alternatives.

But the solution actually being proposed is quite different, consisting of three strategies:

- Increase the exploitation of coal-bed methane, a source of natural gas that is expensive and environmentally destructive (the production process entails a waste stream of saline, toxic water that pollutes water tables and streams).
- Open up access to lands not now accessible because of environmental and other restrictions.

- Import more liquefied natural gas (LNG) from suppliers overseas, including countries like Russia, Bolivia, Iran, Egypt, Algeria, Nigeria, and Venezuela.

It is clear that the first two options will not solve the problem. Increasing the extraction of coal-bed methane can at best soften the decline of natural gas availability in North America because of the limited total recoverable amount available (about 100 Tcf, or five years' supply at current rates of natural gas usage, according the optimistic assessment of the USGS).[24] And even with the most liberal permitting processes and the lifting of environmental regulations, new domestic conventional natural gas sources offshore or in Alaska cannot hope to keep production flat, because of the long lead time needed for the building of drilling and pipeline infrastructure. Deep-water production in the Gulf of Mexico provides about 3 billion to 4 billion cubic feet of natural gas per day, and could yield somewhat more — but Americans now consume about 65 billion cubic feet of gas each day.

LNG has the long-term potential to increase gas supply to North Americans, since global gas extraction will, depending on economic circumstances, continue to increase for as many as 20 years (global gas discovery peaked in 1980). But this strategy is problematic for other reasons. Natural gas is currently not traded internationally to the same extent as oil, because the latter is so much easier to transport by ship. For the most part, gas is extracted and piped regionally. In 2003, the US had only four LNG offloading terminals and shipped gas made up only three percent of US supply. LNG tankers, which must keep the liquefied resource at -260 degrees Fahrenheit (-160 C), are expensive to build — as are gas offloading terminals — and the existing fleet is already spoken for through contracts to supply Japan, South Korea, and China.

Tremendous investment and considerable lead time will be required to build the infrastructure to make gas from overseas a significant part of the US supply picture, yet by the time the infrastructure is in place and working, a global peak in natural gas production may well be imminent.

Nevertheless, speaking December 17, 2003 to energy ministers from 18 producer countries and private sector representatives, US Energy Secretary Spencer Abraham called on natural gas-producing countries to step up to the challenge of creating an "immense" global gas industry. He said that these countries and natural gas importers must work together to develop new fields, build new LNG terminals, expand LNG fleets, and enter into "mutually beneficial," long-term agreements to satisfy growing global demand for natural gas.[25]

Energy Secretary Abraham appears to be proposing a global trade in natural gas similar to the global oil trade that has resulted over the past several decades in worsening energy dependence, economic insecurity, and geopolitical instability. This hardly seems prudent.

My colleague Julian Darley has produced an excellent summary of the situation in his book, *High Noon for Natural Gas,* in which he writes:

> [T]he US will find the world of LNG potentially much more troubling than that of oil, which it did so much to create. To the extent that the so-called "War on Terror" is a cover for increasingly desperate moves to control the world's dwindling oil supply, expanding into LNG, with its mainly Muslim production sources, threatens the planet with an even greater likelihood of endless war, covert disruption, and forced regime change.[26]

Thus the deepening supply problem in North America is set to become a global nightmare.

A Perilous Prosperity

Hydrocarbons have been both the greatest blessing and the greatest curse our species has ever encountered.

Coal, oil, and natural gas have given us the industrial revolution — planes, trains, automobiles, plastics, synthetic chemicals . . . the list seems endless. They have also brought global warming, pollution, habitat destruction, and modern industrial-scale warfare.

This deep intertwining of benefits and costs makes the problem of fossil fuel depletion especially knotty. When I speak to engineers about this subject, they inevitably tend to see it in abstract terms and in isolation from its ecological context: the problem is that we are running out of oil, therefore the solution must be to discover a new energy source capable of substituting for fossil fuels. Simple!

Since the publication of *The Party's Over* I have received dozens of phone calls, e-mails, and letters from intelligent, well-meaning people with new ideas for alternative energy sources. A few of these proposals appear to be workable, at least on a small scale. Yet rather than becoming a cheerleader for this or that energy alternative, I persist in drawing these people's attention back to the need to reduce population and resource usage. I continue to say that, unless we dramatically cut back our demand on the Earth's life-support systems, a new energy source will make little difference. To the practical problem-solvers this seems blatantly unfair: I have outlined a problem (oil depletion) and they have proposed what seems to them an answer. I must appear to *want* to see the human project go down in flames.

The difference between the engineers' perspectives and mine is that I am viewing the situation as an *ecological* problem — not as an economic or engineering one. While fossil fuel depletion is a real and immediate crisis, it is also symptomatic of a universal ecological dilemma, which consists of three interrelated factors:

1. Population pressure
2. Resource depletion
3. Habitat destruction.

Every species encounters this dilemma from time to time and in one way or another, and we humans have done so in countless ways throughout our tenure on Earth.

There are six possible responses to the ecological dilemma:

1. Move elsewhere (i.e., find territories that are under-exploited).
2. Exploit existing resources more intensively (many human technologies, including fire and agriculture, provide ways of doing this).
3. Discover new exploitable resources (uranium and so on).
4. Limit population (tribal cultures have accomplished this in the past through sexual taboos, infanticide, prolonged lactation, birth control, or other measures).
5. Limit resource usage (e.g., through ethical systems that valorize voluntary poverty).
6. Die off (usually from famine, disease, or predation).

The first three options are "supply-side," while the latter three focus on the "demand side" of the survival equation. For other species, supply-side options are usually limited, and so demand-side responses predominate. For example, when deer overpopulate the woodlands of the American Midwest, their numbers are eventually culled through starvation and predation (including hunting by humans).

Our species, in contrast, has become extraordinarily good at finding and implementing supply-side solutions to the ecological dilemma. We have populated virtually the entire surface of the Earth; we have invented new technologies (including plows, steam shovels, and stock exchanges) to exploit resources more intensively; and we have harnessed new resources (from aluminum to zinc) to temporarily enlarge our environment's carrying capacity. The current global human population level is a testament to our ingenuity. (See Chapter 1, pages 19–32, of *The Party's Over* for a lengthier description of the supply-side strategies that humans have developed over the millennia.)

But our very success brings grave problems.

Because nature cannot tolerate the unlimited proliferation of any species, supply-side strategies are always temporary, and sometimes counterproductive, eventually resulting in spectacular population crashes in species that have momentarily benefited from them.

That is why the solution to the problem of oil depletion cannot consist merely of the development of an alternative energy source. Much of our usage of energy goes to facilitate the extraction, transformation, and use of other resources — metals, soils, water, and so on. Without an accompanying demand-side response, merely increasing the supply of energy to our species will mean the continued depletion of other resources, more competition for those dwindling resources, and an eventual crash. It is our reluctance as a species to undertake demand-side solutions to the ecological dilemma — and not merely our inability to find a suitable substitute for oil — that is leading us toward collapse. Yes, we need to make the transition away from fossil fuels, but we must do so in the context of a concerted effort to reduce the size of our population, the scale of our economic processes, and our impacts upon the biosphere. Otherwise we are merely briefly forestalling the inevitable. (I will return to this point in Chapters 3 and 4.)

We are in deep trouble, and it is essential that we *understand* the nature of the trouble we are in. Once we have done so, we must examine our options. It is to the latter task that we turn now.

In each of the next four chapters we will explore a category of options available to us as a species during the next century. These are not options in a narrow, technical sense — as in how we might heat our houses next year, or how we might get better gas mileage in our cars. They are, rather, options in a broad, systemic sense. What can we do, what should we do — as a species, and as individuals — if we are indeed living in the early collapse phase of the greatest civilization ever known? As we are about to see, the stakes are high and our choices are already rather tightly constrained.

CHAPTER TWO

Last One Standing

The Way of War and Competition

Iraq can be seen as the first battle in the Fourth World War.

—James Woolsey, former CIA chief, November 2002

How is the world most likely to respond to energy resource depletion in the decades ahead? One possible answer: *with increased competition for the remaining resources* (especially oil and natural gas), leading, in the worst-case scenario, to the general destruction of human civilization and most of the ecological life-support systems of the planet.

That is, of course, a breathtakingly alarming prospect. As such, we might prefer not to contemplate it — except for the fact that considerable evidence attests to its likelihood.

The notion that resource scarcity often leads to increased competition is certainly well founded. This is generally true among non-human animals, among which competition for diminishing resources typically leads to aggressive behavior. Animal combat seldom results in fatalities; however, when resources become extremely scarce fatal encounters do occasionally occur, especially among carnivores.

Fatal competition for resources among humans is much more readily documented.

Many scientists and philosophers have wondered why aggression between members of the same non-human species over territory, food, dominance, and sexual rights rarely leads to death, while human conflicts, epitomized by war, often do. The answer, apparently, has to do with social behavior and intelligence. Humans, using language, cooperate to secure resources for their group — which is the unit of survival. We humans are also toolmakers, and many of our tools are designed specifically to hurt or kill. In animal combat within a single species, non-life-threatening wounds usually (though not always) discourage one of the fighters before death occurs; in human combat, however, weapons can quickly inflict fatal wounds: a fighter is often killed before he can back down. In addition, human intelligence concerns itself with planning for the future. If a defeated foe lives to retreat, he may return to fight another day; thus the human warrior may go out of his way to kill his enemy in order to avoid having to confront him again later.

In his authoritative study, *Warless Societies and the Origin of War,* anthropologist Raymond C. Kelly notes that, in even the simplest human societies, wars are often fought over resources.[1] As an example, Kelly summarizes ethnographer A. R. Radcliffe-Brown's 1930s description of two Aboriginal Australian tribes: ". . . when a party of collectors or hunters of one tribe arrived at a shellfish bed, honey tree, or hunting ground to find a party of hunters or gatherers of the other tribe already in place, a conflict ensued in which . . . the larger group took possession of the contested resource by force of arms." In his book, Kelly documents the evolution of organized combat from simple raids and revenge killings to state warfare involving thousands of fatalities. Motives for war appear to remain fairly constant throughout social evolution, but the *scale* of the violence has steadily increased over the past several millennia, in tandem with the size of the societies involved and with the levels of their technology.

An article in the May/June 2003 issue of *Archaeology* by Stephen LeBlanc of Harvard's Peabody Museum confirms that "human prehistory was dominated by wars usually over critical resources such as hunting grounds, water, and good cropland. Too many people in one region meant all might starve, so each tribe tried to drive others farther away . . . . [P]rehistoric wars often killed up to 25 percent of the males along with large numbers of non-combatant females."[2]

The most deadly conflict on American soil, in terms of fatalities as a percentage of population, was probably King Philip's War of 1675–1676, fought between Puritan colonists and the Wampanoag nation of Native Americans. The conflict resulted largely from resource disputes: Europeans, in purchasing land from the Indians, assumed that all use rights were transferred; the Natives, however, believed that they were merely permitting the colonists to live on the land, and still expected to retain resource rights (e.g., for hunting and fishing) forever. As the Pilgrims built more fences, resources that the Natives required for survival became unavailable. The ensuing war resulted in horrific casualties on both sides, and in the permanent devastation of the way of life of the native peoples of New England.

Since the 17th century, population densities in North America and elsewhere have increased dramatically, as has sophistication of weaponry. Students of recent political and military history see competition for resources as a component in most of the significant conflicts of the modern era, including both World Wars — in which rivalry over access to oil reserves played no small part. While few modern wars have resulted in a percentage of casualties as high as that in King Philip's War (among the Wampanoags, there were 150 deaths per 1,000 individuals, versus 20 per 1,000 among the US population in the American Civil War), deaths in absolute numbers have been unprecedented (roughly 50,000,000 in the World War II — or about two percent of the global population — versus 3,800 in King Philip's War).

No conflict in the past century has exceeded World War II in scope. But if another general non-nuclear war were to occur, casualty figures could well far surpass those of the most lethal 20th century wars. A nuclear war could conceivably result in the deaths of billions.

Can the Free Market Prevent Resource Wars?

It could be argued that the eruption of a general war over energy resources during the next century is unlikely for two reasons: first, replacements for oil will be available; and second, the global market provides a context in which war for control over resources no longer makes sense.

I will address the first argument — that oil will soon cease to be an important resource — in more detail in Chapter 4. For the moment, it is necessary only to point out that oil is clearly a vital resource now, and according to national and international planning agencies (including the US Department of Energy and the International Energy Agency) it is likely to remain our primary energy source for at least the next three decades.

But what about the market argument — that war cannot rationally be used to control resources in a world in which everything is already for sale?

This line of thinking was recently used by several commentators to counter the idea that the US invaded Iraq in 2003 to gain access to that country's sizeable oil reserves.[3] Let us say that the US did indeed wish to have the oil of Iraq: why spend tens of billions of dollars invading the country and taking over its petroleum industry? After all, Iraq's oil already was, and will continue to be, for sale on the international oil market. Why not just *buy* the stuff? Today, with Iraq under US military occupation, its oil is still up for sale to the highest bidder: there is no pipeline leading from Baghdad directly to Houston. In fact, because of the war and its chaotic aftermath, as of this writing, *less* is available for sale than was the case prior to the invasion. If the war had been undertaken to loot Iraqi oil, the effort was evidently overwhelmingly counterproductive. Today, the argument goes, it is just not practically possible for one country, however militarily powerful, to directly drain off another country's resources, bypassing the mechanisms of international commerce.

This is a persuasive line of reasoning on the face of it, but it ignores the realities of how markets really work. If the global market were in fact able to prevent resource wars, the past half-century should have been a period of near-perfect peace. But resource disputes have instead erupted repeatedly, and continue to do so. Just in the past twenty years, resource disputes have erupted over oil in Nigeria, Algeria, Colombia, Yemen, Iraq/Kuwait, and Sudan; over timber and natural gas in Indonesia (Aceh); and over copper in Bougainville/Papua New Guinea — and this is far from being an exhaustive list.

In classical economic theory, all actors within a market system act rationally in pursuit of their own interests, and no one buys or sells without an expectation of benefit. In the real world, however, buyers and sellers enter the marketplace with unequal levels of power. Some economic players have wealth and weapons, while others don't; as a result, some have figurative — if not literal — guns to their heads persuading them to act in ways that are clearly *not* in their own interest.

Lest we forget: the essence of the European colonial system was the maintenance of unequal terms of trade through military duress. While nearly all of the old colonial governments were overthrown after World War II in favor of indigenous regimes, much of the essential structure of colonialism remains in place. Indeed, some would argue that the new institutions of global trade (the World Trade Organization, together with lending agencies like the World Bank) are just as effective as the old colonial networks at transferring wealth from resource-rich poor nations to militarily powerful rich consuming nations, and that the failure of these institutions to enable the fair distribution of resources will ultimately result in a *greater* likelihood of armed conflict within and between nations.

The new post-colonial international system works to maintain and deepen inequalities of wealth primarily through control (on the part of the wealthy, powerful nations) over the rules and terms of trade, and over the currencies of trade.

During the colonial era, this control was blatant. European powers like England, Spain, and Portugal bled their colonies for resources and cheap labor at the point of the sword. Adam Smith explained the process as follows:

> A small quantity of manufactured produce purchases a great quantity of rude produce [i.e., raw resources]. A trading and manufacturing country, therefore, naturally purchases with a small part of its manufactured produce a great part of the rude produce of other countries while, on the contrary, a country without trade and manufactures is generally obliged to purchase, at the expense of a great part of its rude produce, a very small part of the manufactured produce of other countries.[4]

Consider the example of India. Prior to its colonization by Britain, India was an exporter of fine muslins and luxury fabrics. The British invaded, banned textile imports from India, and heavily taxed the textile trade within that country. As a result, British cloth came to dominate the Indian market. Other industries were dealt with similarly. Under British rule, India produced only cheap raw materials such as indigo, jute, and poppies, while being forced to import manufactured products its citizens were prevented from making for themselves.

The last Indian export item mentioned above — poppies — serves to highlight even further the role of the military in colonial trade. In the late 18th and early 19th centuries, British traders introduced opium, made from Indian poppies, into China. After seeing the social results of opium addiction, the Chinese government banned importation of the drug. Britain went to war with China on two occasions to enforce "free trade" in opium, seizing Hong Kong in the process.

After World War II, as former colonies gained independence, wealthy industrial nations learned to dominate global trade through more subtle methods. Many efforts toward "development" in fact served as bait for a debt trap, in which banks actively pressed cash-strapped third-world governments to accept loans that had to be repaid, with interest, in the same currency as the loan itself (usually US dollars), thus forcing the borrowing nation to export resources or hire out its labor force at a discount to obtain foreign funds. Often the lender stipulated that the money be used to contract with Western firms for projects such as dam building, or to buy equipment — including weaponry — from Western manufacturers. Thus much of the loan money quickly returned to first-world economies; much of the rest was often siphoned off by corrupt officials in the borrowing nation. Meanwhile, first-world technology was held as proprietary (intellectual property), so that prohibitive royalties prevented third-world nations from entering into competition in the profitable high-tech and pharmaceutical industries. When poor countries could no longer afford interest payments on loans, the World Bank and International Monetary Fund imposed "structural adjustment" programs that entailed the selling off to Western corporations of national resources and whole public-sector industries — telecommunications systems, postal systems, waterworks, and sewage systems, for example.

Since money is (among other things) a claim on resources, the ability to control the currency of exchange can itself effect a subtle ongoing transfer of real wealth — often more effectively, easily, and cheaply than can direct military conflict. The US has benefited enormously from the fact that, for the past half-century, its dollar has been the international currency of account for nearly all nations, and since 1975 has been the currency with which oil-importing nations must pay for their fuel. Currently, if any country wishes to obtain dollars with which to buy oil, it must sell its goods or resources to the US, take out a loan from a US bank (or the World Bank — functionally the same thing), or trade its currency on the open market and thus devalue it. America's massive trade deficit effectively constitutes a huge, constantly expanding, interest-free loan from the rest of the world.

Within this new global system, the US thus plays a unique role both because of the preeminence of its currency, and because of its function as military enforcer acting on behalf of the entire international capitalist system. American military intervention is often symbolic, intended to show what can happen to any nation that chooses to ignore the system's rules. Intervention is, however, typically a last resort: more cost-effective means of control include covert actions to overthrow troublesome governments or to install puppet leaders. The US has militarily removed (or attempted to remove) regimes in Vietnam, Iraq, Guatemala, Nicaragua, Grenada, Panama, Afghanistan, Yugoslavia, Libya, and Angola; and has used covert action against governments in Iran, Chile, Greece, Venezuela, and elsewhere. Some of these governments were totalitarian, others democratic; in some, populist leaders sought to distribute resources to their people rather than funnel them to the international business elite; in others, puppet dictators became too greedy and outlived their usefulness.

So: the idea of a truly free market is a fiction — probably as much so now as at any time in history. To be fair, it is true that economists sometimes admit that the free market is an unrealized ideal; but as such it has little to do with historical, political, and social reality. Rather than the market making resource wars obsolete, war (or the threat of war) is actually an integral part of the modern market system. Further, to the degree that the market creates or exacerbates economic inequality (and economic inequality has clearly increased markedly during the past two decades of global market mania), it makes conflict ultimately more likely, as extreme economic inequality either must be sustained by overt or threatened violence, or it will be opposed by violence.

The Case of Iraq

Earlier, I cited the example of the recent US invasion of Iraq as a point of contention with regard to the likelihood and efficacy of resource wars. *Was this war indeed about oil?*

The question gains force because it is now clear that the *ostensible* reasons for the invasion were the product of a systematic campaign of deceit. Indeed, the Bush and Blair administrations have become embroiled in scandals over demonstrable lies told to "sell" the war to their respective legislative bodies, news media, and populations. But was the war, then, an effort simply to steal Iraq's petroleum, as some war critics asserted?

Today, as noted earlier, Iraq's oil is sold on the international market, just as it was prior to the invasion; theoretically that oil is just as likely to end up in Tokyo or Shanghai as in Chicago or Los Angeles. Thus it is indeed unlikely that American and British motives were to simply commandeer Iraqi oil outright. However, one cannot help but wonder whether the US and Britain would have expended so much financial and diplomatic capital to invade Iraq if that country were not a key to the future of the international oil trade. If, instead of having the world's second-largest oil reserves, Iraq were the world's foremost exporter of, say, kumquats, would America be spending tens of billions of dollars to "liberate" its citizens?

It is possible to glean some evidence about American motives from policy documents issued before the war. One document, titled "Rebuilding America's Defenses: Strategies, Forces And Resources For A New Century," was written in September 2000 by the neo-conservative think-tank, Project for the New American Century (PNAC), for Dick Cheney, now vice president, Donald Rumsfeld (defense secretary), Paul Wolfowitz (Rumsfeld's deputy), George W. Bush's younger brother Jeb, and Lewis Libby (Cheney's chief of staff). The document calls for the creation of a "global Pax Americana," and notes that:

> The United States has for decades sought to play a more permanent role in Gulf regional security. While the unresolved conflict with Iraq provides the immediate justification, the need for a substantial American force presence in the Gulf transcends the issue of the regime of Saddam Hussein.[5]

Another document, a report titled "Strategic Energy Policy Challenges For The 21st Century," was commissioned by Dick Cheney, chair of the White House Energy Policy Development Group, from the Baker Institute for Public Policy, a think-tank set

up by former US secretary of state James Baker. The report, issued
in April 2001, concludes:

> The United States remains a prisoner of its energy
> dilemma. Iraq remains a de-stabilizing influence to . . .
> the flow of oil to international markets from the Middle
> East. Saddam Hussein has also demonstrated a willing-
> ness to threaten to use the oil weapon and to use his
> own export program to manipulate oil markets.
> Therefore the US should conduct an immediate policy
> review toward Iraq including military, energy, econom-
> ic and political/diplomatic assessments.[6]

Further, it is now known (as the result of a FOIA suit by Judicial
Watch) that the Report of the Cheney Energy Task Force, issued in
March 2001, contained a map of Iraqi oilfields, pipelines, refineries,
and terminals, as well as two charts detailing Iraqi oil and gas projects,
and a discussion of "Foreign Suitors for Iraqi Oilfield Contracts."[7]

Together, these suggest that the invasion was likely conceived
long in advance — probably prior to the 9/11 attacks — and served
several purposes. Primary among these were the demonstration of
US military power within this strategically important region, and
the establishment of permanent military bases in order to deal
proactively with increasing instability in Saudi Arabia and other oil
exporting countries.

Identifying US motives requires understanding the larger context.

The US needs oil; its wealth was built on energy resources, but
the nation imports well over half of what it uses. In order to maintain its global dominance, the US needs to be able to ensure stable
oil imports at stable prices. And the US has made it clear that it will
use force toward that end. Saudi Arabia, the world's foremost producer, opens or closes the spigot in order to control price swings.
According to British documents released in January, the United
States considered using troops to seize oil fields in Saudi Arabia and
Kuwait during the oil embargo by Arab states in 1973 (when Soviet

Russia threatened to intervene in the war on the side of the Arabs, US President Richard Nixon put US forces on worldwide nuclear alert, bringing the superpowers nearer nuclear conflict than at any time since the 1962 Cuban missile crisis); and the Carter Doctrine of 1979 explicitly states that the US will use its military to maintain access to the oil supplies of the Middle East.[8]

Today Saudi Arabia teeters, beset by a growing and youthful population, dwindling per-capita incomes, and simmering Islamist radicalism. In the years ahead, the power of the Arab oil producers can only grow, since non-OPEC, non-Russian oil production is peaking now and will soon begin its inevitable decline.

Given this context, it is not difficult to guess the true objectives of the Iraq invasion (though guess we must). The thinking must have gone something like this: If the US were to install a compliant puppet regime in Baghdad — or divide Iraq into smaller, more tractable Turkish (Kurdish), Sunni, and Shi'ite autonomous zones — it could break the back of OPEC. It could at the same time begin to replace Saudi Arabia as the swing producer (and thus controller of world oil prices) with a compliant Iraq, and build permanent bases in the latter country, just across the border from the world's largest oil fields. The cost of the effort would be offset by the sale of Iraqi oil on the world market. Soon the entire Middle East could be cowed into compliance with US objectives.

What of the argument that the invasion of Iraq had to do with containing radical Islamist terrorism? America does indeed fear al Qaeda and similar groups — though the relationships between the US and the Islamists is deeply complex, since many of these groups are in fact creatures of previous US covert activity.[9] But what is the source of those groups' current conflict with the US? Osama bin Laden and his followers have stated that they want the US out of the Middle East, but the US cannot abandon the region because of the strategic importance of its oil reserves. The US administration was thus likely speaking truthfully when it said that the Iraq invasion had to do with its war on terrorism — but only in the sense that the war on terrorism is also, at its core, a war over energy resources.

Another reason for the invasion likely has to do with maintaining dollar hegemony. In November 2000, Iraq announced that it would no longer accept dollars for its oil, and would accept instead only euros. Since then, other oil-exporting nations, including Iran and Venezuela, have stated that they are contemplating a similar move. In July 2003, Malaysia proposed switching from quoting oil prices in dollars only to quoting them in dollars and euros; Russia has floated a similar idea. If OPEC as a whole were to change from dollars to euros — as it has recently suggested it may do — the consequences to the US economy might be catastrophic. Investment money would flee the country and real estate values would plummet.

Since the invasion, Iraq has resumed selling its oil for US dollars only.

Thus the invasion and occupation of Iraq were probably envisioned as effectively giving the US a voting seat in OPEC or undermining OPEC; while placing new American bases within hours' striking distance not only of Saudi Arabia, but of Iran and Syria as well; while also helping forestall the collapse of the dollar and hence the US economy.

The outcome of the Iraq invasion does not, at the time of this writing, appear encouraging for many of these objectives: the chaotic conditions under the new puppet regime in Baghdad give evidence of strategic miscalculation, mishandling of intelligence data, and an arrogant style of diplomacy that has alienated former allies. So far, the US has succeeded primarily in demonstrating the lethality of its weaponry. CIA analysts are leaking warnings that the country may be on a path toward civil war, while US plans to quickly transfer sovereignty to a transitional government are mired in controversy.

While Mr. Bush has declared that the world is now safer as a result of the invasion, the case can certainly be made that the region is actually much less stable than it was before, and that further conflicts — ongoing violence in Iraq, instability in Saudi Arabia, deepening strife in Israel/Palestine, and clashes between the US and Syria or Iran — are now more likely than was the case previously.

Just When We Need Brilliant Leadership . . .

But that is actually putting the matter too mildly. In the Introduction, I promised some straight talk, and, with regard to the current US administration, plain language is in order. My main message in this chapter is that military and strategic competition for resources is made likely by the very nature of our circumstances, and thus transcends the policies of a specific party or administration. However, one cannot overlook the particulars: when power is concentrated in few hands and decisions carry immense implications, a simple personality quirk or character flaw can mean a great deal. With regard to the Bush crew, we are dealing with much worse than quirks or flaws.

I believe that the neoconservatives now in power are extraordinarily dangerous people, by any historical measure. I do not say this as a political partisan; in my view, the opposition Democrats are for the most part themselves corrupt and incompetent. I hold little hope that they, or the Greens, could fully solve the immense problems facing the US at this point. However, it seems to me that the current administration goes far beyond the levels of corruption and incompetence that Americans have come to expect from their elected leaders in recent decades. In four short years, Bush, Cheney, and company have managed to do the following:

- **Steal an election.** The means by which Bush and Cheney gained office were profoundly subversive of the democratic process. Florida, under the direction of governor Jeb Bush, had illegally purged its voter rolls of thousands of eligible voters, most of them Democrats. At the time the vote count was halted by a highly politicized decision of the US Supreme Court, Bush was ahead by a mere 300 votes. Had the election been conducted legally, there is no doubt that Al Gore, who led by half a million votes nationwide, would have become president.[10]

WHO ARE THE NEOCONS?

Neoconservatism is the intellectual offspring of Leo Strauss (1899-1973), a Jewish scholar who fled Hitler's Germany and taught political science at the University of Chicago. According to Shadia Drury in *Leo Strauss and the American Right,* (Griffin, 1999), Strauss advocated an essentially Machiavellian approach to governance. He believed that:

- A leader must perpetually deceive those being ruled.
- Those who lead are accountable to no overarching system of morals, only to the right of the superior to rule the inferior.
- Religion is the force that binds society together, and is therefore the tool by which the ruler can manipulate the masses (any religion will do).
- Secularism in society is to be supressed, because it leads to critical thinking and dissent.
- A political system can be stable only if it is united against an external threat, and that if no real threat exists, one should be manufactured.

Drury writes that "In Strauss's view, the trouble with liberal society is that it dispenses with noble lies and pious frauds. It tries to found society on secular rational foundations."

Among Strauss's students was Paul Wolfowitz, one of the leading hawks in the US Defense Department, who urged the invasion of Iraq; second-generation students include Newt Gingrich, Clarence Thomas, Irving Kristol, William Bennett, John Ashcroft, and Michael Ledeen.

Ledeen, a fellow at the American Enterprise Institute and author of *Machiavelli on Modern Leadership: Why Machiavelli's Iron Rules are as Timely and Important Today as Five Centuries Ago* (1999), is a policy advisor (via Karl Rove) to the Bush administration. His fascination with Machiavelli seems to be deep and abiding, and appears to be shared by his fellow neocons. "In order to achieve the most noble accomplishments," writes Ledeen, "the leader may have to 'enter into evil.' This is the chilling insight that has made Machiavelli so feared, admired, and challenging. It is why we are drawn to him still ...."

Machiavelli's books, *The Prince* and *The Discourses,* constituted manuals on amassing political power; they have inspired kings and tyrants, including Mussolini, Hitler, Lenin, and Stalin. The leader, according to Machiavelli, must pretend to do good even as he is actually doing the opposite. "Everybody sees what you appear to be, few feel what you are, and those few will not dare to oppose themselves to the many, who have the majest of the state to defend them .... Let a prince therefore aim at conquering and maintaining the state, and the means will always be judged honourable and praised by everyone, for the vulgar is always taken by appearances ...." It is to Machiavelli that we owe the dictum that "the end justifies the means."

In her essay "The Despoiling of America," investigative reporter Katherine Yurica explains how a dominant faction of the Christian Right, which she calls "dominionism," has found common cause with the neoconservative movement. Dominionism arose in the 1970s as a politicized religious reaction to communism and secular humanism. One of its foremost spokespersons, Pat Robertson (religious broadcaster, former presidential candidate, and founder of the Christian Coalition), has for decades patiently and relentlessly put forward the view to his millions of daily television viewers that God intends His followers to rule the world on His behalf. Yurica describes dominionism as a Machiavellian perversion of Christianity. For the Christian right, neoconservatives like George W. Bush and John Ashcroft can do no wrong, because they are among God's elect. All is fair in the holy war against atheists, secular humanists, Muslims, and liberals.

- **Place criminals and human-rights violators in prominent policy-making positions.** As a result of former President Reagan's Contra war against Nicaragua, the United States became the first country in history to be convicted of international terrorism in a world court tribunal and to be condemned by the United Nations. Several key Reagan administration officials were indicted or tried in connection with the massive human rights violations that occurred in Central America during the Contra war. In the early months of the G.W. Bush presidency, several of these officials were given prominent new jobs: Elliott Abrams, who was convicted of lying to Congress in the Iran-Contra scandal, was appointed National Security Council (NSC) Special Advisor on Democracy, Human Rights, and International Operations. John Poindexter, the mastermind behind the Iran-Contra scam (guns for hostages), had been found guilty of conspiracy, obstruction of justice, and destruction of evidence; he was made Director of the Information Awareness Office (IAO), a new agency "to counter attacks on the US." John Negroponte, whom rights groups charge with covering up political killings and purging information from embassy human rights reports that implicated the military and CIA in disappearances of civilians, became US ambassador to the UN. Other criminals and purported human-rights violators appointed to high posts included Roger Noriega, John Maistro, and Otto Reich.[11]
- **Facilitate a terrorist attack on the US in order to consolidate political power.** In my previous book I resisted taking a clear public stand regarding government complicity in the 9/11 attacks, but, after spending countless hours sifting the evidence, I find the conclusion inescapable: persons within the US government had clear foreknowledge of the attacks, and efforts to prevent those attacks were systematically thwarted on orders from higher levels. Many warnings had been received by the US government that a terrorist attack would occur in the

week of September 9 — some specifying that commercial airliners would be hijacked and that the World Trade Center and
Pentagon would be targeted. Then, after the hijackings
occurred, no fighter jets were dispatched to intercept the airliners, despite the fact that there was plenty of time for this to
have occurred, and that it is standard procedure. There are
many other holes in the official version of the events, too
numerous to discuss here. And finally, the administration has
engaged in public — and largely successful — efforts to prevent or limit any serious inquiry into the 9-11 attacks. In short,
lines of evidence point to foreknowledge, complicity, and
cover-up at the top levels of government. These are extraordinary assertions, and they require extraordinary evidence to
support them. The detailed presentation and discussion of that
evidence is beyond the scope of this book; however, I have
appended print and online resources. See especially David Ray
Griffin's *The New Pearl Harbor* (Interlink, 2004).[12]

- **Lie to the American people and the world in order to justify the illegal invasion of a sovereign nation.** Again and
again, the administration cited Iraq's continued possession of
weapons of mass destruction as the reason for the invasion.
Iraq permitted UN weapons inspectors back into the country
in the waning months of 2002, but this step was deemed
insufficient, so great and immediate was the threat from that
country's alleged nuclear weapons and remote-controlled
delivery systems. As of this writing, it is abundantly clear that
Iraq had no weapons of mass destruction and that administration officials knew this but deliberately concocted
"evidence" with which to sell the invasion to the gullible
American public.[13]

- **Undermine the system of international law by proclaiming
the validity of a policy of pre-emptive attack.** We have yet to
see the ultimate fallout from this brazen action. The neoconservatives in charge of American foreign policy have essentially
put forward the view that the US is above international law.

The Bush administration has refused to join the World Court and has undermined existing conventions on chemical weapons, landmines, and nuclear weapons. The unprovoked invasion of one sovereign nation by another (of Iraq by the US and Britain) is a direct violation of the UN Charter; indeed, it is exactly the sort of behavior the UN was established to prevent. In addition, the United States' actions with regard to prisoners held at Camp Delta at the Guantanamo Bay naval station have directly violated the Geneva Conventions: the prisoners are being held as "unlawful combatants," a term with no meaning in international law. By asserting unique rights, immunities, and privileges, the US has alienated the rest of the international community. Eventually, such behavior will cause other nations to form political and military alliances to oppose US hegemony. While the US has the military capability of defeating nearly any individual foe, it cannot subdue the rest of the world working in concert. And economically, America is in a far weaker position than it is militarily: if only a few key nations were to cease supporting US trade deficits and government borrowing, the results would be catastrophic. Unilateralism sets the stage for a battle that America cannot win; indeed, it is one that the entire world is certain to lose.

- **Use weapons that kill indiscriminately — i.e., "weapons of mass destruction" — in the invasions of both Afghanistan and Iraq.** While time has shown that Saddam Hussein did not possess banned weapons, the Americans and British did possess indiscriminately lethal and possibly illegal weapons, and proceeded to use them — as they had done in the 1991 Gulf War and (with other NATO forces) in the former Yugoslavia. The UN has sought to ban both depleted uranium munitions and cluster bombs (the US has objected), and a recent UN report stated that these weapons breach several international conventions.[14] Some allege that hundreds of thousands of Iraqis and Afghanis, and tens of thousands of American soldiers, have been sickened or killed by DU weapons, which disperse radioactive particles throughout the battlefield land-scape. Each M1 tank round consists of ten pounds of uranium-238, which vaporizes into a highly toxic aerosol upon impact. Much of Iraq is now covered with tons of the stuff. Major Doug Rokke of the US Army, who was assigned by the Army in 1990 to assess the health effects of DU ammu-nition, told a Palo Alto audience in April 2003 that "When I did their research, [I found out] that you can't use [DU muni-tions] because you can't clean up and you can't do the medical." According to Rokke, the effects of DU on American soldiers themselves have been horrific (so much for support-ing our troops); but for the land and people of the nations we are "liberating," DU carries far longer-term consequences: soil and water are poisoned virtually forever. In May, 2003 a *Christian Science Monitor* correspondent took a Geiger count-er to areas of Baghdad that had been subjected to heavy shelling by US troops and found radiation levels 1,000 to 1,900 times higher than normal. To be fair, it should be emphasized that DU munitions had been deployed prior to the advent of the Bush administration; however, these weapons' continued and expanded use (between 1,100 and 2,200 tons used during the 2003 invasion of Iraq versus 300 tons in the 1991 Gulf War and 10 tons during the bombing of Serbia in 1999), in a war fought ostensibly to prevent another nation from using banned weapons, is a bitter irony.[15]

- **Subvert the US Constitution.** Since September 11, 2001, the Bush administration, the US Justice Department, and Congress have enacted a series of Executive Orders, regula-tions, and laws that have seriously undermined civil liberties and the checks and balances that are essential to the structure of democratic government. The framers of the US Constitution sought to prevent any one branch of govern-ment from accumulating excessive power. By using Executive Orders and emergency interim agency regulations as standard tools to combat terrorism, the Executive branch has chosen methods largely outside the purview of both the legislature and the judiciary. Many of these Executive Orders and agency regulations violate the US Constitution and the laws of the United States, as well as international and humanitarian law. In addition, these actions have been shrouded in a cloak of secrecy that is incompatible with democratic government. Hundreds of non-citizens have been rounded up and detained, many for months, in violation of constitutional protections, judicial authority, and INS policy. The government has repeatedly resisted requests for information regarding the detainees from loved ones, lawyers, and the press; it has denied detainees access to legal representation; and has conducted its hearings in secret, in some cases denying the very existence of such hearings. In a democracy, the actions of the government must be transparent, or our ability to vote on policies and the people who create those policies becomes meaningless.

Perhaps the most disturbing aspect of the government's actions has been its attack on the Bill of Rights, the very cornerstone of American democracy. The War on Terror has seriously compromised the First, Fourth, Fifth, and Sixth Amendment rights of citizens and non-citizens alike. From the USA Patriot Act's over-broad definition of domestic terrorism, to the FBI's new powers of search and surveillance, to the indefinite detention of both citizens and non-citizens without formal charges, the principles of free speech, due process, and equal protection under the law have been seriously undermined. At the time of this writing, three states and 246 counties, towns, and cities (including New York, Los Angeles, and Chicago) have passed resolutions, ordinances, or ballot initiatives condemning, or refusing local cooperation with enforcement of, the Patriot Act.[16]

This is an extraordinary performance by any measure. In the current Bush administration we see a combination of gross incompetence, high criminality, and almost limitless power — and this in the context of a time that requires the deftest and most visionary of leadership if we are to avert or at least minimize ecological and human catastrophe. It is difficult to overstate the peril inherent in such a combination. These people will not easily be unseated: if they stole one election, why not another? And if various legal battles threaten to overtake them, why would they not resort to facilitating another "terrorist" incident as justification for declaring martial law? In an interview in November 2003, former US General Tommy Franks, who led America's campaigns in Afghanistan and Iraq, stated that if a WMD attack were to hit the US, the Constitution probably would not survive: "the Western world, the free world, loses what it cherishes most, and that is freedom and liberty we've seen for a couple of hundred years in this grand experiment that we call democracy."[17] Was Franks giving us a heads-up on what is in store?

Meanwhile the American people are so "dumbed down" by television that they have little or no awareness of what is happening to them. The media have been engulfed by corporate mergers, and reporters prostrate themselves for access to official military and Executive Branch "sources." The result? For years, studies such as those by University of Massachusetts' Center for Studies in Communication, have shown that people who get their news primarily from television are not only poorly informed, but often seriously misinformed.[18]

The Bush crew's incompetence, so abundantly on display in their handling of the economy and the Iraq invasion, will eventually do them in. But in the meantime they may take the nation, and perhaps the world, down with them. They have one thing going for them: they understand oil depletion at least to some extent, and they understand that the US is about to descend into economic chaos. This is knowledge that few others possess, and it is knowledge that makes them bold. Perhaps they feel that they have nothing to lose. Within their twisted ideological framework, their agenda of global resource domination and domestic repression makes perfect sense. And that agenda can have only dreadful consequences.

WHAT *SHOULD* HAVE BEEN
George W. Bush's Speech to the Nation,
9/11/2001

My fellow Americans, today our nation suffered an unspeakable tragedy when hijackers turned civilian airliners into missiles. This is a critical moment in our nation's history and we must respond with care and conviction.

First, we must mourn the dead and care for the wounded.

Second, we must find, apprehend, try, and punish the surviving members of the conspiracy that perpetrated this horrible act.

Third, we must learn everything we can from and about this terrible crime. We must conduct an open, public investigation into every aspect of the events: Why did the buildings in New York collapse? Why were jet fighters not immediately scrambled to pursue the hijacked airliners? And were there prior links between American intelligence assets and the hijackers themselves?

Finally, we must do what we can to insure that nothing like this ever happens again. It is already clear that the hijackers were of Middle Eastern origin. America's presence in the Middle East has been predicated on our need to import ever-greater quantities of oil. We must reexamine that dependence on foreign resources, and the policies that flow from it.

Our nation became wealthy from oil, but three decades ago our oil production began a historic decline. New oil discoveries have dwindled, and it is clear that domestic oil production will continue to decrease in the future, until we have effectively run out of this precious resource. Since our nation's oil production peak in 1970, we have attempted to maintain our energy-dependent way of life by importing more and more oil from elsewhere. But it is becoming ever clearer that, unless America weans itself from foreign energy resources, we will be drawn deeper into a quagmire of attack and counterattack, of colonial wars and of economic turmoil from unpredictable prices. We can change this trajectory, and we must, but to do so will require effort from every one of us.

We will all be called upon in the days ahead to sacrifice. If we, the people of this great nation, will join together in a shared work of national transformation and renewal, our children will thank and praise us.

To be fair, the sacrifice and effort required must be shared as equally as possible. Those who have benefited most from the economic miracle of cheap energy must contribute the most to the great transition ahead: I am speaking now of the oil companies, the automobile companies, the armaments manufacturers, and the airline industry. Our great corporations and wealthiest individuals must show the way.

It would be easy to underestimate the magnitude of the task before us. Our economy — our very way of life — is bound up with oil and petroleum products. Finding substitutes and ways to do more with less will take ingenuity and hard work. However, in the end there is no choice. Just as oil production has peaked and declined in our country, it will soon do so for the world as a whole. We can choose to prepare for that day now, or we can wait, becoming ever more dependent on other nations, in which case we will become ever more vulnerable.

If we take up this great challenge today, we can lead the world by example rather than by force of arms. The events of the past twenty-four hours can be a great wake-up call, not only to our own nation, but the world as a whole. If by the end of this decade we have succeeded in cutting our fossil fuel consumption by half, and are on the way to making a similar reduction in the following ten years, we will preserve the world's climate while laying the groundwork for global peace and stability. I can think of no greater legacy for our children, and no more fitting memorial for those who were needlessly killed today. May their deaths not have been in vain.

Types of Resource Wars

The Iraq invasion was, of course, a unique event, precipitated by unique circumstances and involving unique political actors. It is important to understand the specific event and its context, but it is also important to keep in view the larger trends. Let's step back a moment and again look at the bigger picture. To what extent is the Iraq invasion indicative of the kinds of resource conflicts that might erupt in the decades ahead?

Iraq is actually the nexus of several different kinds of conflict — between consuming nations (e.g., France and the US); between

THE PENTAGON PREPARES FOR RESOURCE WARS IN A CLIMATE-RAVAGED WORLD

In its February 9, 2004 issue, *Fortune* magazine featured an article summarizing a Pentagon report that discusses security implications for a hypothetical future world running amuck because of severe climate change. In *The Pentagon's Weather Nightmare,* David Stipp begins by asking the reader to "Imagine Eastern European countries, struggling to feed their populations, invading Russia — which is weakened by a population that is already in decline — for access to its minerals and energy supplies. Or picture Japan eyeing nearby Russian oil and gas reserves to power desalination plants and energy-intensive farming."

Stipp goes on to summarize the Pentagon's assumptions and conclusions: dramatic climate change is possible, and thus the US military needs to prepare contingency plans for a long era of icy temperatures in Europe and North America, intense storms, and massive drought that leaves billions of people struggling for the necessities of existence.

A follow-up article by Ira Chernus ("Pentagon Goes Crazy for Massive Climate Change") on the <www.commondreams.org> website quoted from the report itself: "History shows that whenever western industrial nations and "terrorist" groups (ones not previously based in Iraq, but playing an increasing role in the region); between factions within Iraq itself (Kurds, Shi'ites, and Sunnis); and — most obviously — between a powerful consuming nation and a weaker, troublesome, producing nation.

It is useful to disentangle these various kinds of conflict, so that we can begin to sort the types of resource wars that are already in progress, and that are likely to erupt in the future:

humans have faced a choice between starving or raiding, they raid"; therefore we should assume that, if the world undergoes dramatic climate change during the next few decades, "an ancient pattern [will re-emerge]: the eruption of desperate, all-out wars over food, water, and energy supplies . . . . Warfare may again come to define human life."

The good news is that "The U.S. is better positioned to cope than most nations," having more "wealth, technology, and abundant resources." There is a downside to this, however: "It magnifies the haves-vs.-have-nots gap and fosters bellicose finger-pointing at America."

The US strategy should be to "build a fortress around itself to preserve resources." The nation's borders would have to be "strengthened to hold back starving immigrants from Mexico, South America, and the Caribbean islands," since "waves of boat people pose especially grim problems."

The report describes this as a "no regrets strategy" that will enable the US to survive "without catastrophic losses."

<www.fortune.com/fortune/technology/articles/
0,15114,582584-3,00.html>

<www.commondreams.org/views04/0202-02.htm>

(a) Between powerful consumer nations and weaker, resource-rich nations. History — especially that of the colonial period — is filled with examples of this type of conflict. US interventions — whether direct or covert — in Venezuela, Iran, and Colombia are of this type. As energy resources become more scarce and valuable, future conflicts appear likely between the US and various nations in the Middle East, Africa, and South America. Even Canada may have cause for concern as competition for dwindling North American natural gas intensifies, though an actual invasion seems unlikely any time soon.

(b) Civil wars. This kind of conflict is most likely to erupt within resource-rich nations, as competing groups vie for shares of the wealth. Civil wars have recently been fought over control of exportable resources in Angola, Congo, Myanmar, Peru, and Cambodia. Future civil conflicts over domestic energy resources are likely in Saudi Arabia, Iraq, and Colombia.

(c) Between consuming nations. Market mechanisms have historically been relatively successful in allaying this kind of conflict, as long as the supply of the resource in question is sufficient to meet demand. However, when absolute scarcity arises, conflict among consumers becomes more likely. Twice in the twentieth century Germany went to war in order to gain colonies, territory, and energy resources. China is currently the world's second-biggest oil importer (after the US); its imports grew 32.8 percent just during the first half of 2003. At some point, the amount of oil available on the export market will be insufficient to meet the demands of both nations. What happens then? Direct military conflict seems unlikely, but the competition is sure to be fierce and will probably take a variety of forms. The market solution to insufficient supply is "demand destruction," which usually entails raising prices until some potential buyers simply abandon the market. However, there are other possible forms of demand destruction — including covert sabotage of competing nations' economies.

(d) Asymmetrical war, or "terrorism." Warfare does not always take conventional forms. When a rich nation seeks violently to control poor resource-rich nations, it may not be able to prevent the violence from spilling over into its own territory. Properly defined, "terrorism" is violence perpetrated against civilians for political ends. Both states and non-state political organizations perpetrate terrorist acts, though the term itself has become highly politicized, and it is usually only non-state violence that is so labeled by the press or official spokespeople. As resources fall further into dispute, both state and non-state terrorism are likely to become more common.

Conflicts over resources can have secondary effects, including economic hardship resulting from the destruction of infrastructure, and the diversion of national wealth into support for an expanding military. Some nations may institute domestic political repression as a way to deal with "terrorism" or dissent (itself provoked by the funneling of increasing shares of financial and other resources toward the military and away from basic services).

The Path of Least Resistance

None of this is to say that resource wars are inevitable. As we will see in the next chapter, there are clear alternatives to conflict. Still, the prospect of an increase in the frequency and intensity of resource wars in the next few decades represents not just a potential *worst-case* scenario, but rather the *default* scenario.

That is because dealing with resource shortages with competition and conflict may be easier politically than any alternative. As we will see shortly, avoiding conflict will entail cooperation and voluntary self-restraint — and the latter conflicts with both the need for continued economic growth and with the desires of most citizens for a more abundant future. Conflict, on the other hand, merely requires demonizing the opponent. Politicians may thus find it easier to persuade their constituents to fight a common enemy than to conserve and share.

CHINA AND THE US:
INTERDEPENDENT COMPETITORS

Just over a half-century ago, when an emerging Asian power felt constrained by its need for more energy, the consequences were catastrophic. The US imposed an oil embargo on Japan in 1941 to halt the latter's aggression in East Asia, and Japan responded by attacking Pearl Harbor.

Today Japan remains an important industrial producer, but it is China whose energy appetite is causing concern in the corridors of power around the world. China's economy is growing at a phenomenal eight to ten percent a year, compared to the rest of the world's three percent growth; as a result, China's consumption and imports of most metals and minerals has escalated substantially in the past few years.

Last year, auto sales in China grew 70 percent, while its oil imports increased 30 percent from the previous year, making the nation the world's second foremost petroleum importer after the US. By 2030, China is expected to have more cars than the US and to be importing as much oil as the US does today. In December 2003, China's biggest city, Shanghai, banned bicycles on its largest avenues: while bicycles carried more than 70 percent of travelers in Shanghai as recently as 1990, they are used by only 15 percent of commuters now. In 2003, the voracious Chinese economy was responsible for one third of the world's growth in oil demand, with 60 percent of China's oil imports coming from the Middle East.

Until just a few years ago China was self-sufficient in oil. However, the Daqing oilfield — by far the nation's largest — produced just 50.1 million tons in 2003, down from a peak of 56 million tons in 1997. This oilfield in northeastern Heilongjiang province, developed in the late 1950s, is expected to produce only 30 million tons a year by 2010.

Meanwhile, the nation is experiencing severe and recurring fuel scarcities: in 2003 several provinces suffered diesel fuel shortages, and supplies of gasoline were also tight. Major Chinese electricity producers have run badly short of coal and have appealed for state intervention to solve the shortage, which has gravely hampered normal electricity production.

As a way of feeding its rapidly increasing energy appetite, China seems to have set its sights on neighboring countries, with a focus on Russia and Central Asia. However, the Middle East, as the site of 70 percent of the world's petroleum resources (according to official figures), also seems to be of intense interest to Chinese policy makers. A report by the US-China Economic and Security Review Commission, a group created by Congress to monitor American-Chinese relations, warned in 2002 that China was increasingly providing technology and weapons components to Iran, Iraq, and Syria, and that "this arms trafficking to these regimes presents an increasing threat to US security interests in the Middle East." The report concludes: "A key driver in China's relations with terrorist-sponsoring governments is its dependence on foreign oil to fuel its economic development. This dependency is expected to increase over the coming decade."

Yet at the same time, globalization has made the US and China almost inextricably dependent on each other: China depends increasingly on US food exports, while the US depends on cheap Chinese manufactured goods. China's own food production is declining rapidly, and the US is one of the few nations still exporting food surpluses. China runs a trade surplus of over $100 billion a year with the US, and with its foreign exchange earnings, China has been buying huge quantities of US Treasury securities (as of January 2004, roughly $190 million per day), thus helping the US to maintain its debt burden. China also buys nearly $50 million a day in mortgage-backed bonds from US home-lending agencies Freddie Mac and the FNMA ("Fanny Mae"). In effect, China sells Americans cheap goods, and then lends the money with which to buy them.

In many instances, mutual dependency makes for stable international relations. However, when the pattern of dependency is asymmetrical, or when it is disrupted by a scarcity of needed goods or raw materials, a tense period of readjustment — perhaps including warfare — can result.

War is always grim, but as resources become more scarce and valuable, as societies become more centralized and therefore more vulnerable, and as weaponry becomes more sophisticated and widely dispersed, warfare could become even more destructive than was the case during the past century.

By far the greatest concern for the future of warfare must be the proliferation of nuclear weapons. Today, the US and Russia together have over 12,000 nuclear weapons. Twelve nations have nuclear weapons programs at some stage of development, with Iran, Brazil, and North Korea recently making efforts to join the nuclear club. Moreover, the US is conducting research into new types of nuclear weapons — bunker busters, small earth-penetrators, etc. — that are designed to be used in battlefield situations. The US has come close to using nuclear weapons 14 times since World War II, when it became the first and — so far — only nation to employ them against a civilian target. Recent US administrations have enunciated a policy of nuclear first-strike.[19]

Chemical and biological weapons are of secondary concern, although new genetic engineering techniques may enable the creation of highly infectious and antibiotic-resistant "supergerms" capable of singling out specific ethnic groups.

Additionally, the US has announced its intention to maintain clear military superiority to any potential rival ("full-spectrum dominance"), and is actively developing space-based weapons and supersonic drone aircraft capable of destroying targets anywhere on the planet at a moment's notice. It is also developing an entirely new class of gamma-ray weapons that blur the critical distinction between conventional and nuclear weapons.[20]

Despite the US's aspirations to dominance, the September 11, 2001 attacks — though evidently facilitated by the Bush administration — clearly demonstrated the vulnerability of America to lightly armed but highly motivated groups determined to inflict damage to a centralized urban infrastructure. If increasing competition for the world's dwindling energy resources represents the path of least resistance, then we are in for a long, tough ride. It is impossible to say where, when, or how the spiral of violence will end.

Perhaps a clear understanding of the consequences of this path of action can render the alternatives — however politically difficult — nevertheless more compelling. Thus, it is to the alternatives that we turn next.

CHAPTER THREE

Powerdown

The Path of Self-Limitation, Cooperation, and Sharing

*Keeping the [global economic] bubble from bursting
will require an unprecedented degree of international
cooperation to stabilize population, climate, water tables,
and soils — and at wartime speed. Indeed, in both scale
and urgency the effort required is comparable to the
US mobilization during World War II.*

—Lester R. Brown, *Plan B* (2003)

If the consequences of "Last One Standing" are unthinkable, then what other path might we take?

If humankind is to avoid ruthless competition for dwindling energy resources, coordinated efforts toward cooperation and conservation will be needed: The ways in which this could be achieved are probably limitless, but the broad-scale options are likely few and easily surveyed. Industrialized societies would have to forego further conventional economic growth in favor of a costly transition to alternative energy sources. All nations would have to make efforts to limit per-capita resource usage. To avoid competitive struggle, powerful countries would have to reduce disparities of wealth both among their own people, and also between themselves and poorer nations. Not only would oil, coal, and natural gas need to be conserved, but also fresh water, topsoil, and other basic and limited resources. Moreover, as energy available for industrial transportation declines, economies would have to be unlinked from the global market and re-localized. Everyone — especially those in rich, industrial nations — would have to undertake a change in lifestyle in the direction of more modest material goals more slowly achieved. And inevitably, with the conservation of resources would come the necessity to stabilize and reduce human populations.

Until now, most efforts toward the elimination of global conflict have centered on creating mechanisms for arms control and conflict resolution. In order to avoid resource wars, we would need more such mechanisms; but in addition, we would need to address the *ecological* conditions for peace. If population pressure and resource depletion are predictable causes of antagonism between and within societies, then avoiding deadly competition would seem to require low population levels relative to the available resource base.[1] Peacemaking would thus entail not only negotiation, but resource and population management on a global scale.

In short, Powerdown would mean a species-wide effort toward self-limitation.

Many people are already comfortable thinking along these lines; environmentalists have long championed societal self-limitation in various forms. Usually the argument is framed in ethical terms: we should limit population and industrial/economic growth for the sake of future human generations or to enable other species to survive.

However, other people are quite *un*comfortable with the Powerdown scenario, precisely because it would threaten economic growth. This view is also expressed in moralistic terms: our only hope of supporting our large and burgeoning population (its advocates say), is to grow the economy and to invest heavily in new technology and scientific research. To limit scientific progress would be to crush the human spirit and doom millions to poverty; while to limit population growth would require trampling on the most basic of human rights — the right to reproduce.

The ethical case for continued economic growth is compelling if we ignore certain uncomfortable facts — that is, if we assume continued, uninterrupted resource streams. Once the processes and implications of resource depletion are understood, the moral grounding of the pro-growth argument crumbles.

However, it is not only powerful interests that ardently promote the pro-growth position; there are also those who question whether, in principle, Powerdown is even possible. What if systematic self-limitation goes against our biological hardwiring? Could it be that nature has designed us to be competitive, so that all efforts toward compassion and cooperation are doomed to amount to no more than self-delusional strategies to consolidate survival bonds with groups of kin and surrogate kin? In his book *The Selfish Gene,* science writer Richard Dawkins proposed that humans are essentially just genes' tools for reproducing themselves.[2] According to Dawkins and other genetic determinists, all human projects (from the building of civilizations to their destruction in warfare) are just elaborate strategies that human genes have evolved to compete with other human genes. Genuine efforts toward self-limitation, in this view, are anathema to our fundamental purpose as genetic robots, and what appears to be cooperative behavior is actually rooted in deeper, unconscious competitive strategies.

If this is true, then we may as well stop right here. The horrors of the Last One Standing strategy are inevitable, and we or our immediate descendants will probably die in resource wars, famines, or plagues.

However, there are good reasons for thinking that human motives and capabilities are more complex than can be summarized in "selfish-gene" discourse. In the previous chapter we saw that competition for resources is indeed a normal state of affairs in nature. Yet the same can be said for self-limitation, cooperation, and sharing (see sidebar on the following page).

Of course wild animal species as well as humans *do* undergo instances of population bloom, overshoot, and dieoff, and they *do* compete with one another in various ways. Only those who insist on seeing the world through rose-colored glasses would deny that this is so. My point is simply that, for most animals and for humans as well, ruthless competition is only a part of the available behavioral repertoire, which also includes a variety of strategies for *avoiding* overpopulation and overt competition.

POWERDOWN IN NATURE

Animals' strategies for limiting procreation are quite varied; the most widespread mechanisms used by birds and mammals are territoriality and social hierarchies. Foxes provide an interesting example of the latter. During the breeding season, adults usually live in pairs or in small family groups of from two to six. Most groups of more than two consist of a dominant dogfox and vixen, with the remainder of the group including either siblings or offspring. If more than one vixen conceives, usually only the dominant female will give birth; the other pregnant females will typically spontaneously abort their cubs. This behavior is presumably hormonally controlled. If the dominant vixen is for some reason unable to deliver her cubs, one of the subordinate females may then go on to produce a live litter. Even the litter size seems to respond to a self-limiting imperative, with more cubs being produced when regional population density is low and fewer when it is high.

Animals also engage in many kinds of cooperative behavior, both with members of the same species and with those of differing species. The possible examples here are virtually endless, and have been discussed at length by Augros and Stanciu in their book, *The New Biology* (Shambhala, 1987); the authors quote biologist Lewis Thomas as saying that "The urge to form partnerships, to link up in collaborative arrangements, is perhaps the oldest, strongest, and

According to genetic determinists, even apparent instances of cooperation and self-sacrifice are explainable as unconscious competitive strategies based in our DNA. The argument is a complex one, and involves assessing the fitness-related costs and benefits to individuals, distinguishing the interests of groups from the interests of their individual members, and seeing the world from the "genes'-eye view" to reveal how individual fitness interests can overlap. In a way, the underlying motive for observed cooperative or self-limiting behavior

most fundamental force in nature. There are no solitary, free-living creatures, every form of life is dependent on other forms."

Human reproductive self-limitation is common to most traditional societies, as was documented by Richard Wilkinson in his 1973 book *Poverty and Progress,* and typically takes the forms of abortion, infanticide, prolonged breastfeeding, or restrictions on sexual intercourse. Wilkinson wrote:

> If starvation is to be prevented, physiological checks on population size must be supported by cultural ones. Adequate cultural checks only exist in well-adapted societies or, in case that appears to be a tautology, they appear in traditional societies which have established themselves in a way of life undisturbed by European contact or other new influences.

Human cooperative and altruistic behavior is sufficiently common that it is unnecessary to cite examples here. Complex human societies simply could not exist if it were not for ongoing, pervasive cooperative efforts on the part of all concerned. For those interested in reviewing the subject a greater depth I would recommend the anarchist classic, *Mutual Aid,* by geographer and naturalist Peter Kropotkin (1902).

is irrelevant; from our present perspective, as we look for a path of survival in the post-petroleum world of the near future, the important questions are simply whether such behavior is possible, and how to foster it. Whether we save ourselves and our planet because we are fundamentally selfish, or because we are genuinely altruistic and care deeply about other species and future generations, is a question for biologists and philosophers. What is important is *whether we can and do undertake the cooperative efforts necessary to our survival.*

Once we have established that both ruthless competition and self-sacrificing cooperation are available as behavioral alternatives, the question arises: what causes a given individual or community to choose one path or the other in a given instance? Is the choice made by genetic preference (some individuals being more inclined to compete, others to cooperate), by conscious decision, or by circumstance? Without discounting the roles of genes or conscious choice, one can make the case that environmental circumstance is demonstrably a factor in many instances. As Richard Wilkinson pointed out in his 1973 book *Poverty and Progress,* stable social and ecological environments tend to produce self-limiting human societies, while contact with the unstable dynamism of global industrial commerce causes traditional societies to shed their self-limiting cultural behaviors. Something similar can be said for other species: population blooms and competition tend to occur in disturbed environments, or as the result of the introduction of successful invasive species; while stable population levels and cooperative behavior predominate in undisturbed climax ecosystems.

This is not reassuring information. The world of the early 21st century could hardly be characterized as stable, and the planet is quickly running out of examples of undisturbed climax ecosystems. Globalized corporate capitalism prides itself on creating a dynamic, competitive environment. In a thousand ways we have set ourselves up for a grand, punishing game of Last One Standing. If we are to change course and instead pursue a cooperative Powerdown strategy, we will have to alter a great deal about ourselves — how we think as well as how we behave — and do so quickly. This is a tall order by any measure.

We do have one thing going for us. We humans have developed complex cultures based largely on language, and our evolution over the past several millennia has occurred almost entirely at the cultural — as opposed to the biological — level. In order to save ourselves we do not need to evolve new organs; we just need to change our culture. And language-based culture can change very swiftly, as the industrial revolution has shown us.

Thus a Powerdown solution is arguably possible in principle. But what, exactly, would the process look like?

Requirements for Powerdown

In the early 1970s, the Club of Rome commissioned, from a MIT-based international team of researchers led by Donella Meadows, a study on the future of industrial society. Published as *The Limits to Growth* in 1972 (hereafter referred to as *LTG*), the book provoked a debate that is still going on. The study concluded that if prevailing growth trends continued, fundamental resource limits would be reached in the middle of the twenty-first century, leading to a dramatic, uncontrollable collapse of population, food production, and other significant measures of social viability.

Several economists have attempted to debunk the conclusions presented in *LTG*. For example, in *Eco-Scam: The False Prophets of Ecological Apocalypse*, Ronald Bailey wrote that "In 1972, *The Limits to Growth* predicted that at exponential growth rates, the world would run out of gold by 1981, mercury by 1985, tin by 1987, zinc by 1990, petroleum by 1992, and copper, lead, and natural gas by 1993."[3] *Facts not Fears: A Parents Guide to Teaching Kids about the Environment* by Michael Sanera and Jane S. Shaw repeated part of this list and pointed out that "The world did not run out of gold by 1981, or zinc by 1990, or petroleum by 1992, as the book predicted."[4]

However, these were not predictions contained in the book. The reference for these claims is Table 4 (pages 56 to 59) in *LTG*. The table lists three sets of numbers: a static reserve index (how long known reserves would last at 1972 rates of consumption); an exponential reserve index (how long known reserves would last at an exponentially increasing rate of consumption); and an exponential index calculated using five times the known reserves (that is, assuming substantial new discoveries of the resources in question). Criticisms of *LTG* focused only on the second, "exponential reserve" set of numbers, which was the most pessimistic, even though the authors clearly stated that this did not constitute a prediction, but merely a statistical extrapolation:

> Of course the actual nonrenewable resource availability in the next few decades will be determined by factors much more complicated than can be expressed by either the simple static reserve index or the exponential reserve index. We have studied this problem with a detailed model that takes into account the many interrelationships among such factors as varying grades of ore, production costs, new mining technology, the elasticity of consumer demand, and substitution of other resources.[5]

In fact, rather than having been refuted or debunked, the *LTG* study has withstood the test of time quite well and is widely regarded as an early landmark in the literature on sustainability.

While the main message of *LTG* was worrisome, the book's second important conclusion was that it might be possible to establish a state of global equilibrium in which society would be "sustainable without sudden and uncontrollable collapse" and "capable of satisfying the basic material requirements of all of its people."[6] What would be required to achieve this? The authors listed seven recommendations:

1. Stabilize the human population (which, in 1970, stood at about 3.6 billion).
2. Increase efficiency, so that "resource consumption per unit of industrial output is reduced to one-fourth of its 1970 value."
3. Shift economies from production of goods to provision of services.

4. Reduce pollution "per unit of industrial and agricultural output" to one-fourth its 1970 value.
5. Divert capital to food production so that the entire population is fed.
6. Shift agriculture to a sustainable model (e.g., using compost as opposed to chemical fertilizers) to avoid soil depletion.
7. Improve the design of industrial goods to maximize durability and repairability.[7]

I have described the contents of *LTG* in some detail because both its analysis and its recommendations clearly framed the terms of the discussion that we must now take up in earnest. Two updated volumes have appeared in the interim, using new statistics (*Beyond the Limits*, in 1992, and *The Limits to Growth: The 30 Year Update* in 2004).[8] By 1992, the authors had reached the conclusion that "overshoot [can] no longer be avoided through wise policy; it [is] already a reality"; and in their latest contribution, they note that they "are much more pessimistic about the global future than we were in 1972. It is a sad fact that humanity has largely squandered the last 30 years in futile debates and well-intentioned, but half-hearted, responses to the global ecological challenge."[9]

One brief trend in the sustainability literature was the suggestion that individual, small-scale initiatives would be sufficient to turn the tide. Perhaps the most familiar example of this trend was the best-selling *50 Simple Things You Can Do to Save the Earth* by the Earthworks Group (GK Hall, 1989), which offered suggestions for recycling, reusing, bicycling, and insulating homes. However, the book soon provoked a response, in the forms of *50 Difficult Things You Can Do to Save the Earth* (by Gar Smith, Earth Island Journal Press, 1995), and *Simple Things Won't Save the Earth*, by J. Robert Hunter (University of Texas Press, 1997). The point being made by these critics was that the unsustainability of industrial society is due not just to individuals' decisions about product choice and personal behavior, but to fundamental socioeconomic structures, institutions, and processes. Some writers went even further: as Garrett Hardin pointed out in his widely-discussed essay "The Tragedy of the Commons," efforts toward self-limitation on the part of a few, undertaken in a competitive environment, are predictably futile and

KYOTO AND BEYOND

The Kyoto Protocol is an initial step toward global Powerdown: while intended as a solution to global climate change, it effectively also addresses the problem of energy resource depletion.

Negotiated in 1997, the agreement mandates a reduction in the emission of greenhouse gases (principally carbon dioxide, which is produced from the burning of fossil fuels) to levels 5.2 percent below those in 1990; this is to be achieved by industrial countries by the year 2012. Non-industrial nations would be exempted for the moment, though negotiations are intended to begin soon on cuts to be made by the developing world.

While Europe has embraced Kyoto in principle, the US — which emits more greenhouse gases than any other country — has refused to ratify the protocol. In December 2003, Russia likewise appeared to decline ratification of the document "in its present form," though that nation has yet to declare its official position.

As a result, some policy analysts have concluded that Kyoto is dead; others, however, point out that some European nations are already seeking to live up to the spirit of the Protocol, and that even if this particular agreement is never fully implemented, the nations of the world will eventually be forced to come up with something similar.

Critics of Kyoto fall into two camps: those who complain that implementation will curtail economic growth (especially in the developed nations); and those who say that the mandated emissions reductions are insufficient (some climate scientists say that cuts of up to 80 percent by mid-century will be needed in order to avert catastrophic climate change).

Alternative proposals exist. Ross Gelbspan, author of The Heat Is On (Perseus, 1998), has proposed instead a World Energy will result simply in the marginalization of self-limiters and the exhaustion of commonly available resources.[10]

Modernization Plan, which relies on three primary strategies:

- Change energy subsidy policies in industrialized nations.
- Create a large fund to transfer renewable energy technologies to developing nations.
- Replace the emissions trading scheme in the Kyoto framework with a progressively more stringent Fossil Fuel Efficiency Standard.

Meanwhile Tom Athanasiou and Paul Baer, authors of *Dead Heat: Global Justice and Global Warming* (Seven Stories Press, 2002), defend the basic structure of Kyoto and argue that equity issues are of core importance in dealing with climate change. The northern, industrial nations have benefited from fossil fuel use; southern "developing" nations are unlikely to forego similar benefits willingly. Thus, avoiding climate catastrophe will require northern nations to fund a huge renewables-based development program in the south. Athanasiou and Baer suggest a post-Kyoto treaty based on a North-South compromise along the following lines:

- Insist on the industrial nations' responsibility for climate change.
- Recognize that the costs will be high and that increased energy efficiency will not by itself be enough.
- Allocate tradable emissions rights on an equal per capita basis, which would be modified to take account of differing national circumstances to increase fairness.

Athanasiou and Baer predict that "business as usual" will inevitably lead to "barbarism and the fortress world." Instead, they envision a "great transformation" that "melds the imperatives of poverty alleviation and ecological protection with traditional and radical democracy to yield something strong and fine and new."

THE UPPSALA PROTOCOL
— *Proposed by Uppsala Hydrocarbon Depletion Study Group, Uppsala University, Sweden*

WHEREAS the passage of history has recorded an increasing pace of change, such that the demand for energy has grown rapidly over the past 200 years since the Industrial Revolution;

WHEREAS the required energy supply has come mainly from coal and petroleum formed but rarely in the geological past, such resources being inevitably subject to depletion;

WHEREAS oil provides 90 percent of transport fuel, essential to trade, and plays a critical role in agriculture, needed to feed an expanding population;

WHEREAS oil is unevenly distributed on the Planet for well-understood geological reasons, with much being concentrated in five countries bordering the Persian Gulf;

WHEREAS all the major productive provinces had been identified with the help of advanced technology and growing geological knowledge, it being now evident that discovery reached a peak in the 1960s;

WHEREAS the past peak of discovery inevitably leads to a corresponding peak in production during the first decade of the 21st Century, assuming the extrapolation of past production trends and no radical decline in demand;

WHEREAS the onset of the decline of this critical resource affects all aspects of modern life, such having political and geopolitical implications;

WHEREAS it is expedient to plan an orderly transition to the new environment, making early provisions to reduce the waste of energy, stimulate the entry of substitute energies, and extend the life of the remaining oil;

WHEREAS it is desirable to meet the challenges so arising in a cooperative manner, such to address related climate change concerns, economic and financial stability and the threats of conflicts for access to critical resources.

NOW IT IS PROPOSED THAT

1. A convention of nations shall be called to consider the issue with a view to agreeing an Accord with the following objectives:

a. to avoid profiteering from shortage, such that oil prices may remain in reasonable relationship with production cost;
b. to allow poor countries to afford their imports;
c. to avoid destabilising financial flows arising from excessive oil prices;
d. to encourage consumers to avoid waste;
e. to stimulate the development of alternative energies.

2. Such an Accord shall have the following outline provisions:

a. No country shall produce oil at above its current Depletion Rate, such being defined as annual production as a percentage of the estimated amount left to produce;
b. Each importing country shall reduce its imports to match the current World Depletion Rate.

3. Detailed provisions shall be agreed with respect to the definition of categories of oil, exemptions and qualifications, and scientific procedures for the estimation of future discovery and production.

4. The signatory countries shall cooperate in providing information on their reserves, allowing full technical audit, such that the Depletion Rate shall be accurately determined.

5. Countries shall have the right to appeal their assessed Depletion Rate in the event of changed circumstances.

It would be reassuring to think that we could save the Earth if only each of us were to make one small contribution each day. But the challenging reality is that making human society sustainable will require a large-scale reform of governments and economic systems, and the use of mechanisms of authority to apply penalties and offer incentives.

In a discussion of systemic hurdles to sustainability in *The Party's Over*, I cited an example that is worth mentioning again here. Many environmentalists have argued that the constant push for economic growth within industrial societies is one of the engines continually straining global resource limits (this point is brilliantly discussed by Richard Douthwaite in his *The Growth Illusion*, New Society Publishers, 1999). However, it would be difficult to remove the growth imperative from modern economies without also changing national monetary systems. That is because currently most money is loaned into existence by banks and is thus based on debt, and implies a commitment on someone's part to pay interest on that debt. If the economy does not grow, new money will not be created to pay interest on existing loans; many of those loans will thus be defaulted upon, and a crash will occur. Thus it is essentially impossible to achieve a static or controllably contracting economy with a debt-based currency.

Therefore, if we are to achieve a reduced-scale, steady-state society, we will need to change our monetary system to one that is *not* based on debt and interest. In principle, this would be quite easy: nations or locales could issue their own interest- and debt-free money instead of giving banking cartels (such as the Federal Reserve, the Bank of England, Deutsche Bank, etc.) legal monopolies on money creation. This is what the framers of the US Constitution envisioned, and debt-free national currencies have existed at various points in American history (e.g., Lincoln's "greenbacks" and Kennedy's "United States Notes"). But in the US (and the situation is similar in most other countries), a permanent shift to debt-free money will require action by Congress, which will itself be problematic as long as senators and representatives are dependent upon campaign contributions for re-election. The banks will likely seek to destroy the career of any politician who attempts to change the monetary system in this way. Thus, the needed reform of our monetary system will first require reform of the political system — itself no easy task.

Meanwhile, it will be necessary for national governments and large economic institutions not merely to cease promoting endless growth, but to implement systemic strategies for increasing efficiency, and for transforming their agricultural and transportation infrastructure. If we are to avoid many of the horrible impacts of energy resource depletion discussed in Chapter 5 of *The Party's Over,* we will have to undertake a World War II-level of collective effort, which can only be marshaled with the help and coordination of government.

In order to alter the consumptive patterns of millions of Americans, public education — call it propaganda if you like — will be required. An effective propaganda system already exists in the form of the advertising and entertainment industries, but that system is currently spreading a message essentially the opposite of what is required. We are all being told daily, in a thousand ways, to buy, consume, and waste; that perpetual growth is both possible and good; that our happiness and welfare depend upon our purchase of ever more consumer goods. The needed message is that we must all reduce consumption, reuse, and repair; and that our happiness and welfare lie in community solidarity rather than the personal accumulation of wealth. The advertising industry will not willingly change its message; nor will the corporations that purchase advertising services gladly reduce the scale of manufacture and distribution of their products, or happily redesign products to increase their durability and reparability. These sorts of changes to the economic system can be realized only through forcible government intervention.

The Paradox of Scale

The perceptive reader will likely already have noted that an effective Powerdown strategy is bound to encounter a nasty paradox. On one hand, the aim of the process must be to reduce the scale of human economic activity, and eventually that of effective political organization. As fossil fuels become less available, globalization based on the intercontinental distribution of resources and manufactured products will contract; ultimately, only a policy of re-localization will permit the survival of a functional social order. At the same time, the modern nation state — which emerged as a political entity during the industrial revolution as the result of growing communications and transportation networks — will likely become unworkable. Political power will necessarily devolve to a local, perhaps bioregional scale.

However, as we have just seen, in the interim it will also be necessary for existing national governments to take forceful and effective charge of their economies in such a way as to preserve social order while reversing the trend of industrial growth; replacing their monetary systems; reducing economic inequality; and supplying public education about sustainability on an immense scale.

Moreover, it will be insufficient to coordinate the Powerdown process merely at the national level; it will be necessary to introduce *international* mechanisms for the coordinated conservation and sharing of remaining resources, for the reduction of population levels, for disarmament, for conflict resolution and negotiation, and for the lessening of economic inequality between nations. International agreements along these lines will require mechanisms of enforcement. What I am suggesting goes far beyond the mandate of the United Nations, or of other international bodies such as the World Bank or World Trade Organization (these latter bodies in fact serve primarily to promote further globalization and inequality, and would thus need to be dismantled or substantially redesigned).

How can governments grow in power and scope . . . in preparation for relinquishing power and reducing their scope? Seen in perspective, the task is paradoxical, and is breathtaking in its complexity and difficulty. We need a reversal not only of industrial growth, but of the trend of increasing centralization of government — even as that trend continues to its logical conclusion.

As a personal aside, I would mention that I have reached these conclusions with great reluctance. I have long been attracted to the philosophical anarchism of Tolstoy and Thoreau, believing that large coercive political and economic institutions are anathema, and that individual liberty and communal solidarity are the paths toward ecological and social sanity. It pains me to think that vigorous action on the part of vast national and global institutions will logically be required in order to avert an Armageddon scenario of resource wars. But, after considerable thought, I see no other way. I hope someone can prove me wrong.

Institutions do not give up power easily. Thus the idea that we must create *larger and more powerful* governmental bodies *in order to later do away with centralized international and national governments* is clearly problematic. One is reminded of Lenin's vision of the dictatorship of the proletariat, which would (in theory) ultimately fade away as universal communism is realized. The contradiction is as obvious as that inherent in the projects of creating peace through war or promoting economic equality by further enriching the wealthy.

Two arguments can be offered in defense of the plan.

First, it is a logical necessity. As noted at the beginning of this chapter, if humankind is to avoid spiraling resource wars, a Powerdown process will be required. Again, efforts on the part of individuals will be insufficient to realize that process, and so large-scale government intervention will be needed. And yet the ultimate goal of the process must be a world that is organized both economically and politically at the local or regional level, because post-petroleum energy resources will be unable to fuel the long-distance transportation needed to maintain extensive networks of distribution and control. The Powerdown process as described may be difficult or impossible to achieve, but *from a logical point of view, it is undeniably what is needed* if we are to avert the alternative.

Second, in this instance the eventual disappearance of temporary international and national authoritarian political institutions would not be mandated just by ideology (as in Marxist theory), but by physical necessity. As energy availability declines, it will become physically impossible to maintain large-scale political organizations, even in the absence of the will to dismantle them.

Useful Precedents

We have just seen what would be required for a Powerdown scenario. To say that this would be the greatest challenge undertaken by the human species in history would be no overstatement. Is it even feasible?

In the first section of this chapter, we saw that other species and human societies in other times have made efforts toward self-limitation and cooperation; this suggests that Powerdown is possible in principle. But we need more assurance than that. We need to see that *industrial societies* are capable of making the transition to sustainability.

We don't have to look far for examples. During the 1970s and early 1980s, after steep hikes in the price of crude oil, the US and other consuming nations instituted efficiency measures that would have been unthinkable just a few years previously. The US Congress lowered the national speed limit to 55 miles per hour and began to mandate higher fleet fuel efficiencies from automakers. Such measures were dramatically effective: the demand for gasoline, which had increased in every previous decade since the introduction of the automobile, stabilized and, in several years, actually declined. But the effort was limited in scope and duration. As oil prices moderated, speed limits went back up and Americans began buying larger, less efficient vehicles.

It is also instructive to look at the achievements of pre-industrial communities that have bypassed the conventional industrial development model and instead created a low-energy, sustainable infrastructure. The State of Kerala in India is an outstanding example in this regard.

Despite having one of the lowest per-capita incomes of all India and near-zero economic growth, Kerala has achieved high levels of well-being. Life expectancy is ten years longer in Kerala for men and fifteen years longer for women than is the case in the rest of India. Infant mortality rates are far lower than in the rest of the country, and women enjoy high levels of educational attainment, with more female university graduates than male, even in the field of engineering. Much of Kerala's success can be attributed to modest family sizes. Partly as a result of women's expanded social and economic opportunities, voluntary choice has held the average reproduction rate in Kerala at 1.7 grown children per child-bearing woman, which is below the replacement rate. As economist Richard Douthwaite describes it,

> Kerala has developed its traditional culture into one that is much more efficient in its use of resources than the Western one which was proposed as a replacement. As a result, Kerala is far more sustainable than anywhere in Europe or North America. In particular, it does not depend on continuous economic growth to stave off collapse and it is far less dependent on overseas trade.[11]

Still, while Kerala can and should serve as a guiding light for the less industrialized world, North Americans and Europeans need an example of a society that *first* industrialized — at least partially — and *then* had to deal with an energy crash.

Perhaps the most instructive example of this scenario is Cuba.

Following its revolution in 1959, Cuba had become dependent on the Soviet Union for oil as well as grain. Agriculture was collectivized into huge state-owned farms. Factory production and overseas trade increased. Though the US, its powerful neighbor to the north, used both covert and overt means to attempt to overthrow its revolutionary government and ruin its economy, Cuba managed to thrive, producing remarkable achievements in the fields of education and medical care. Its people enjoyed the longest life expectancy, lowest levels of infant mortality, and highest literacy rates in the hemisphere. In 1989, Cuba ranked eleventh in the world in the Overseas Development Council's Physical Quality of Life Index, while the US ranked 15th. While Cuba has only 2 percent of the Caribbean region's population, it was producing 11 percent of the region's scientists. Cuba exported trained doctors — 20,000 of them — to the rest of the world.

These feats carried a cost, which was largely subsidized by the Soviets. The latter bought Cuban sugar at over five times the market rate; they also sold oil to Cuba at a discount so steep that it permitted the Cubans to re-export the oil at a profit. From 1959 to 1989, 85 percent of Cuba's trade was with the Soviet bloc.

Not everyone was happy in the Cuban paradise. Roughly ten percent of the population left at the time of the revolution (including the Mafia and most members of the ruling and owning classes), and those that stayed endured an authoritarian regime and a planned economy that left little opportunity for political dissent or individual entrepreneurial initiative. Still, the majority of the people were proud of their revolution and their national attainments.

In 1989 and 1990, as the Soviet bloc disintegrated, oil and grain imports from Russia plummeted. Cuban trade dropped by over three quarters in a matter of months. Fertilizer and pesticide imports fell by 80 percent, making agricultural production difficult even as food imports vanished. Known officially by the Castro regime as the "Special Period in Time of Peace," this episode in Cuba's history saw the nation slide to the verge of collapse.

Because the Cuban economy was directly controlled by the state, and because there was little economic disparity in the country by this time, the shortages were shared more or less equally. Nearly everyone lost weight, tens of thousands of children were seriously malnourished, and the population adopted a mostly vegetarian diet out of necessity.

Meanwhile, the government responded to the agricultural crisis by distributing collectivized land for private cultivation. Within a few years, Cuban agriculture was transformed from consisting of 80 percent state-run farms to 80 percent employee-owned share-holder enterprises. With petrochemicals no longer available, Cuba went organic. Many Cuban scientists, influenced by the interna-tional ecology movement, had already developed a critique of Cuba's chemical-intensive agricultural system. While their voices had been in the minority (and had often been actively stifled by the authorities), with the advent of the Special Period, these ecologi-cal agronomists were suddenly given free rein to experiment and to redesign the system. Soon Cuba boasted a quarter of a million trained organic gardeners using techniques such as integrated pest management, intercropping, and composting. Agricultural pro-duction was moved closer to the cities to reduce transportation, refrigeration, and storage costs. By 1998, there were over 8,000 officially recognized organic urban gardens in Havana, cultivated by over 30,000 people and covering nearly a third of the available land.

Transportation was also devastated by the cut-off of Soviet oil. Today there are few cars on Cuban roads, but nearly every vehicle is filled with passengers due to an official policy that systematically encourages hitchhiking. Bicycles are common, and animals (espe-cially oxen) are often used both for human transport and for traction in agriculture.

Since human labor is plentiful and energy resources are scarce, the government adjusts salaries to encourage full employment. In many instances, laborers are paid more than managers.

Building materials are in short supply, and so people live in small houses and apartments, most of which are in need of repair. There is little new construction.

US pressure on the Cuban regime has not abated; indeed, it was significantly intensified by the 1992 "Cuba Democracy Act," which tightened the existing trade embargo, and by the cynical-ly-titled 1996 "Cuba Liberty and Democratic Solidarity Act" (also known as the "Helms-Burton Act"), which deters foreign investment.

Nevertheless, Cuba is today able to buy oil at market prices with foreign currency earned through tourism and the export of sugar cane, cobalt, and nickel. One-third of Cuba's oil now comes from Venezuela, whose president, Hugo Chavez, has adopted a friendly stance toward the Castro regime. However, oil imports are still only a fraction of what they were before the Soviet collapse.

Cuba's population of over 11 million is growing, but more slowly than is the case elsewhere in the region. The government has put its emphasis on the development of social capital — the arts, sports, science, and intellectual pursuits — as opposed to the production of material goods, which is necessarily limited. A friend of mine who heads an organization that promotes small communities throughout the US, upon his return from a recent visit to Cuba, remarked, "My organization talks about community, but these people are living it."

Of course, the situation is complex: Cuba still keeps political prisoners, suppresses dissent, and engages in capital punishment; some kinds of food are scarce and the people subsist on a fairly minimal diet; the Cuban economy is largely dependent on tourism; and the nation still imports most of its energy resources.

Nevertheless, Cuba offers us a vision of what our own energy-constrained future *might* look like — given a fairly optimistic scenario. Cuba managed to power down dramatically and quickly, relocalizing its economy with little increase in internal violence, and with relatively little sacrifice in terms of many basic measures of social welfare.

Assessing the Prospects

What lessons can we learn from all of this?

In a positive vein, we might conclude that, when the need arises, change can happen quickly. This was true in the US in the 1970s, and also in Cuba in the 1990s. Apparent cultural blocks to self-limiting behaviors fell away, and people learned to conserve and do things differently.

Today, in the industrialized countries, efforts toward Powerdown are occurring at a snail's pace, despite available evidence that the world's fossil energy reserves are depleting rapidly. This lack of movement is frustrating to those of us who understand what is at stake, but perhaps the apparent complacency will dissipate quickly when actual shortages appear. Current blocks to energy conservation and to a vigorous transition to renewables might vanish virtually overnight if energy prices were to skyrocket, imperiling the economy.

A lesson we might take away from the example of Cuba is that people can do extraordinary things if motivated by a strong and clear appeal to a developed sense of ethics. Most people (though certainly not all) are ethically motivated; they want to believe that what they arc doing is *good*. Ethical systems appear to be an evolutionary mechanism for coordinating human behavior for collective survival, and it is through ethical systems that traditional societies internalize imperatives toward self-limitation. If people feel that a particular behavior is *right,* and are offered cultural support for that behavior, they will do the thing even if it is highly inconvenient or uncomfortable and involves considerable self-sacrifice.

In Cuba, efforts toward Powerdown were ethically mandated from the top down, and the process was facilitated by the fact that, in that country, the Communist party is regarded by most people as the seat of moral authority (it may be difficult for Americans to grasp this, but those who visit Cuba report it as a fact). Most Cubans had confidence that their efforts were not merely enriching a small group of powerful people, and that those making decisions were acting selflessly in service to the whole of society.

In the US, decision makers have squandered much of their moral authority. Polls confirm that most Americans distrust politicians and corporate leaders, and it is easy to see why: CEOs enrich themselves shamelessly at stockholders' (and ultimately the public's) expense, while national and state politicians go begging for money from corporate donors every few years in order to get re-elected. Anyone who pays attention to balance sheets, budgets, and quality news outlets (forget about what passes for news on US television), cannot help but view the American government and economy as suffering from thievery on a colossal scale. And this is occurring in the context of a national ethical system that glorifies competition, regards the accumulation of personal wealth as the foremost goal in life, and assumes that self-sacrifice is for losers. Even many religious leaders in the US (and America is by any measure the most religious of the industrialized nations) promote an ethic that excludes the need for self-limitation from any arena other than that of sex. Thus in order to motivate self-sacrifice and self-limitation on the part of the American people, US governmental, business, and religious leaders would first have to regain the moral standing that they have squandered during the past decades, and then use this standing to fundamentally alter the national mythology and ethic. This *could* be done, but it is no small task.

The examples of Kerala and Cuba are inspiring, but in some ways they are also discouraging. The US isn't Kerala: America is already a highly developed and industrialized nation that is extremely dependent on automobiles, highways, shopping malls, and computers. It is one thing for a traditional society to forego the development of such dependencies; it is quite another for an energy-addicted society to wean itself from the habit.

Nor is the US in the same situation as Cuba: while the people of the latter nation have worked a half-century at building communal solidarity, America is an individualist society. Where Cuba has fostered a cooperative spirit among its populace, Americans are proudly competitive. Yes, when the crunch came Cubans pulled together and carried their nation through a painful economic transformation. But would another country have responded to similar circumstances so successfully? It is relatively easy to think of ones that have met economic challenges with cultural disintegration, deepening corruption or authoritarianism, or internal violence. Recall Germany in the 1920s, or Zimbabwe in recent years.

Finally, it is important to recognize the unique role of the US and China in any potential global effort toward Powerdown. Either country could single-handedly undermine such an effort — China, because of its population and its current drive toward industrialization; the US, because of its immense destructive weaponry, its impact on the global economy, and its belligerent foreign policy.

The US is also uniquely positioned to lead the global energy transition. While it is the world's foremost energy user, the US also possesses advanced renewable-energy research facilities. And China, if it were to follow the model of Kerala or Cuba, rather than attempting to shift its economy in the direction of greater energy-resource dependency, could be a beacon to the less-industrialized nations of the world.

However, currently neither nation is on the path to lead a global Powerdown. Indeed, present trends suggest that the US and China are on a collision course, as the energy appetites of both nations continue to grow in the context of deepening energy-resource depletion.

For the sake of American readers, I will put the matter as bluntly as possible: A peaceful global Powerdown is possible only if the US leads the way. If current American domestic and foreign polices continue, Powerdown efforts on the part of other nations may result in improved survival options for the people of those nations, but for the world as a whole by far the most likely outcome will be devastating resource wars continuing until the resources themselves are exhausted, the human species is extinct, or the fabric of modern societies has been shredded to the point that anarchy — in the worst sense of the word — prevails nearly everywhere.

While a global Powerdown process, in terms of total effort over time, would be extraordinarily difficult and costly, its first stages could be undertaken easily and with minimal sacrifice, merely by mandating increased energy efficiency requirements for US automobiles and electrical power generating facilities, and by offering incentives for the deployment of renewable energy options such as wind, solar, and biomass. Then, as dependency on oil imports was reduced, the military aspects of US foreign policy could be de-emphasized, with a hefty saving of funds that could then be invested in the accelerating transition to a renewable-energy infrastructure. Once such policies were in place, the inevitable impact of fossil-fuel depletion might serve to propel the efforts forward, enabling even deeper systemic changes (such as the transformation of the monetary system and population stabilization and reduction), that now appear politically unthinkable.

It is in this light that we can appreciate the true dimensions of the tragedy of current US political corruption and disintegration. Investments in the status quo on the part of corporations and gov-

NORTH KOREA AS COUNTER-EXAMPLE TO CUBA

Cuba is not the only modern society to have faced an energy famine. North Korea did so at about the same time and for similar reasons, but with very different results. Since the end of the Cold War, North Korea has experienced chronic major shortages of all forms of modern energy supply, with petroleum products, coal, and electricity all falling by over 50 percent after 1990.

Much of the difference between North Korea's and Cuba's responses to energy famine can be attributed to climate and natural disasters: North Korea has a much colder climate than Cuba, and a shorter growing season. North Korea also has less arable land per capita, and what little arable land it has is not of the best quality. Compounding these drawbacks, North Korea has suffered several ruinous natural disasters over the past decade. In 1995 and 1996 floods ruined huge swathes of farmland, sweeping topsoil from hilly areas and depositing silt and sand on valley farmland. In 1995, nearly a million acres (400,000 hectares) of farmland were destroyed just as crops ripened; five million people were left homeless. The flooding also damaged coal mines, electricity generating plants, and transmission lines, adding to the country's energy woes. Floods the following year wiped out 20 percent of the harvest. Then in 1997, the country was hit with a devastating drought that destroyed 70 percent of the corn crop, and a tidal wave deluged over a million acres of rice fields. Another drought struck in

ernmental bureaucracies are preventing efforts that are advocated by everyone who is familiar with the facts. Meanwhile those with the will even to *begin* to change the system are excluded from decision-making positions.

This is a discouraging situation. Nevertheless, it is important that the options and their consequences be clearly outlined and put forward, so that opportunities are not missed simply for lack of awareness.

2000, and was followed that autumn by typhoons and heavy storms. As if this weren't enough, the nation suffered its longest drought ever in 2001, with crop yields reduced by over 50 percent. Hydroelectric plants had to be shut down, and new rice plantings withered. Still another tidal wave struck in October 2001, inundating thousands of acres of rice fields.

The consequences for the people of North Korea of energy shortages, US sanctions, and natural disasters have been horrific. In 1990 the nation produced 8 million tons of grain; in 1996 it produced only 2.5 million tons, and in 2000, only 3.8 million tons — a million tons short of subsistence level. Perhaps as many as 2 million people (out of a total population of 22 million) died during the great famine of the mid-1990s, and much of the population continues to be malnourished. US members of Congress who visited North Korea reported that people were eating grass and bark. Over 60 percent of the children suffer from chronic malnutrition.

The country is still heavily reliant on food aid from international relief agencies; meanwhile, a huge proportion of the nation's yearly budget is devoted to maintaining its army. Renewed famine seems likely as grain production continues to languish, while the generally inept and ruthless government seems to have failed to find permanent structural ways of dealing with energy shortfalls and deteriorating infrastructure. In short, North Korea is probably the most dramatic existing example of a modern industrial society falling into an energy-led collapse.

WHAT CAN WE DO?

Powerdown substrategies are many and varied. Chapter 6 of *The Party's Over* presents a small sampling; Guy Dauncey offers a larger smorgasbord of answers in *Stormy Weather: 101 Solutions to Global Climate Change.* Some samples:

- Join the Cities for Climate Protection campaign
- Buy carbon offsets
- Set up community partnerships
- Introduce a carbon tax and rebate
- Create solar villages

   Other substrategies are being promoted by a range of organizations including:

- The Apollo Alliance <www.apolloalliance.org/>
- The Natural Step <www.naturalstep.org>
- Natural Capitalism <www.naturalcapitalism.org>
- Industrial Ecology <www.is4ie.org>
- Biomimicry <www.biomimicry.org>
- The Global Reporting Initiative <www.globalreporting.org>
- EPRI Eco Solutions <www.earth-assets.com/aboutEA.htm>
- Community Choice <localpower.org>
- The Post-Carbon Institutue <www.postcarbon.org>

Book-length explorations of how the modern world might implement a Powerdown scenario include:

- Hartmut Bossel, *Earth at a Crossroads: Paths to a Sustainable Future,* (Cambridge University Press, 1998)
- Lester Brown, *Plan B: Rescuing a Planet Under Stress and a Civilization in Trouble,* (W. W. Norton, 2003)
- Herman E. Daly and Joshua Farley, *Ecological Economics: Principles and Applications,* (Island Press, 2003)

- Howard Geller, *Energy Revolution: Policies for a Sustainable Future,* (Island Press, 2002)
- Paul Harrison, *The Third Revolution: Population, Environment, and a Sustainable World,* (Penguin, 1993)
- David Holmgren, *Permaculture: Principles & Pathways Beyond Sustainability,* (Holmgren Design Services, 2002)
- Colin Mason, *The 2030 Spike: Countdown to Global Catastrophe* (Earthscan, 2003)
- Howard T. Odum & Elizabeth C. Odum, *A Prosperous Way Down: Principles and Policies* (University of Colorado Press, 2001)

Will any of these solutions actually work? Is there the political will to implement them? Stay tuned.

CHAPTER FOUR

Waiting for the Magic Elixir

False Hopes, Wishful Thinking, and Denial

I'm adamantly opposed to energy conservation. We're not running out. All we have to do is go out and find it and produce it.

— Stephen Moore, President, The Club of Growth

In the best-case scenario, the transition to a hydrogen economy would take many decades, and any reductions in oil imports and carbon dioxide emissions are likely to be minor during the next 25 years.

— National Research Council, "The Hydrogen Economy: Opportunities, Costs, Barriers, and R&D Needs" (2004)

For every expert there is an equal and opposite expert.

— Anonymous

If the Last One Standing strategy is unthinkable and Plan Powerdown is extremely difficult to accomplish, then there must be other alternatives. Surely our options aren't *that* circumscribed, that few, that dismal.

In the question periods that follow my lectures on *The Party's Over*, there are typically comments to the effect that, "You are exaggerating the problem; we have solutions at hand; all we have to do is just . . ." Sometimes the solution mentioned is hydrogen, sometimes it is methane hydrates or free-energy machines. Many of the people making these comments appear to have at least a smattering of technical knowledge. I never feel that my replies are fully satisfactory. I often try to give a thorough explanation of why the particular suggestion offered won't really work to offset all of the awful effects of oil depletion. But this level of detail, so late in the evening, merely serves to tax the patience of the rest of the audience. Moreover, I find myself assuming the uncomfortable role of naysayer. In the body of my lecture I have described an immense quandary — oil depletion — and someone in the audience has proposed something we can do about it. How mean-spirited of me to shoot the idea down!

We humans love to solve problems, and we love to see problems solved. Further, we like to think that every problem has a solution. That humankind has an immense problem that won't easily be solved is a notion that most people would prefer not to entertain.

At the risk of being typecast as a killjoy, I persist. It's a thankless job, but somebody has to do it. Why? Most of the solutions that I hear really *need* to be shot down, because they are deeply flawed in one way or another. We are deluding ourselves by thinking that "All we have to do is just . . .", because even the suggestions that hold merit — like a transition to renewable fuels — actually represent jobs of immense difficulty. Moreover, I'm disturbed when I see large numbers of people happily accept these "solutions" and proceed to file the oil-depletion problem away in a dark corner of memory reserved for "Possible but Unlikely Catastrophes," perhaps in a mental folder adjacent to "Invasion by Space Aliens."

Facile solutions merely draw our attention away from the problem too soon — and we're often quite happy to have our attention so diverted. But then the problem just continues to fester and grow.

Facile solutions are a form of denial. It would be patently foolish to say of some serious threat, "If we ignore it, it will go away"; but we feel absolved of responsibility if a person who sounds authoritative claims to have the problem under control. In that case it is acceptable to turn our attention away.

A particularly pernicious form of facile solution is the kind that *really could work* to solve *the aspect of the problem that presents itself to us*. If we can banish the immediate symptom, why worry about the disease?

In this chapter I intend to answer the persistent "All we have to do is just . . ." suggestions at greater length. It is important to address individual "solutions" honestly and objectively. As we will see, some are actually quite promising in a limited sense. However, we must not allow our excitement over partial answers to cause us to lose sight of the real dilemma that confronts us — which, ultimately, is the fact that there are simply too many of us using too many of Earth's resources too quickly.

I discussed alternative energy sources in Chapter 4 of *The Party's Over*, and I refer the reader to that chapter for a general discussion of the various energy options currently available. In what follows, I aim to update and expand on what I have already written.

Unconventional Hydrocarbon Sources

The simplest replacement for oil would be alternative hydrocarbon sources. Of these, the two mentioned most often are tar sands and methane hydrates. I discussed tar sands in *The Party's Over* (pages 111–112), but since the book's publication that resource has been in the news sufficiently that it deserves further comment here. (By the way, the term "tar sands" is no longer used by the industry, which prefers the more optimistic "oil sands"; I have decided to stick with the older term, as it more accurately describes the nature of the resource.) I did not mention methane hydrates in my previous book, and so that subject certainly deserves discussion here.

In recent years, several companies have invested heavily in the production of synthetic crude from tar sands in the Canadian province of Alberta. The material is a mud-like mixture of sand and clay surrounded by a dense hydrocarbon called bitumen. There are two primary ways of extracting the resource — by mining it with huge shovels and bulldozers, then using steam to separate the bitumen from clay and sand; or by pumping steam underground to "cook" the bitumen over a period of up to two weeks, and then pumping the liquefied bitumen out of the ground.

In 2003, for the first time, Canada decided to report its bitumen as economically recoverable "proven reserves" of petroleum. As a result, with the stroke of a pen, Canada increased its oil reserves by 3,600 percent to 180 billion barrels. This made Canada (on paper) the possessor of the world's second-largest proven oil reserves — after Saudi Arabia, which boasts 256 billion barrels. Canada seemed to have a reasonable justification for its move: the tar sands now provide a third of that country's total crude output.

The increasing exploitation of Canadian bitumen has obvious implications for the oil-peak scenario and even for petroleum geopolitics: if North America now has such vastly increased reserves, why worry about a theoretical impending global oil production peak? And why should the US maintain its dependence on oil from Middle Eastern countries when a friendly country across its northern border reports greater petroleum reserves than those of Iraq?

As I pointed out in *The Party's Over*, while the quantity of tar sands in the ground may be enormous, the *rate of extraction* of that resource will always be limited by the fact that the production process is — and will inevitably continue to be — expensive from both a financial and an energy standpoint, as well as being environmentally disastrous.

Alberta's current output from the tar sands is about one million barrels per day — a significant amount, but only enough to slake about one-twentieth of the total US thirst for crude.

But what is currently required to keep up this level of production? Each day, trucks, motorized shovels, and other heavy equipment remove tons of rock and soil from sites in northern Alberta — enough to fill Yankee Stadium every 48 hours — just to expose the underlying tar sands; the sands themselves must then be mined and hauled to processing plants. There, natural gas and a gasoline-like product called naphtha are used to separate and process the bitumen. These mining projects currently use from 500 to 700 cubic feet of natural gas to produce a single barrel of synthetic crude. The alternate method of "cooking" the bitumen underground — known as "steam assisted gravity drainage" — uses almost twice as much natural gas. Both processes require lots of fresh water.

Prospects for future tar sands production would be rosier if natural gas were more plentiful, but with North American gas production lagging further each month, it seems that tar sands projects are doomed to become increasingly expensive. While the proposed 800-mile Mackenzie Delta gas pipeline project in Canada's Northwest Territories is often cited as a partial solution to North America's natural gas shortages, a 2003 report by Lehman Brothers analyst Thomas Driscoll cautions that nearly all of the gas transported may end up being consumed by tar sands projects in Alberta. What shall we do with our remaining gas — heat our homes or cook bitumen?

It is technically possible to use oil derived from bitumen as a replacement for natural gas in the process of making synthetic crude from tar sands, but the energy profit ratio will inevitably be dismal, and the cost of the resulting crude will be unattractive. This will remain true regardless of increases in the market price of oil.

There may be a lot of hydrocarbon molecules under Alberta's soil, but getting them out of the ground and into American drivers' gas tanks is such an expensive business that we really should continue to consider the tar sands in a category separate from that of conventional crude oil.

❖ ❖ ❖

Methane hydrates represent an even larger store of hydrocarbons in Earth's crust; however, in the end, the prospects for exploiting them may be even more discouraging than is the case with tar sands.

As marine organisms decompose, they release methane. Under certain conditions, that methane can become trapped on the ocean floor in ice crystals, and can build up over time. The resulting mixture of methane and ice is called methane hydrate. This material is also sometimes found in permanently frozen soil on land: there are, for example, methane hydrate deposits in Siberia and Alaska.

Oceanic methane hydrates are so plentiful that, in theory, they could power the world for centuries. Some estimates put the total at more than twice the amount of all other fossil fuels combined.

However, the harvesting of the resource constitutes a technical problem of immense proportions. As hydrate material is mined and brought to the ocean surface, it fizzes and bubbles as methane turns to gas and dissolves in the water. Eventually, the methane makes its way into the atmosphere. The problem then is not merely that a potentially valuable substance has been lost, but that a previously stored greenhouse gas has been loosed on the environment.

The most frequently discussed greenhouse gas is carbon dioxide, which is released with the burning of fossil fuels. However, methane is over twenty times as effective as carbon dioxide at trapping the heat from sunlight. Thus, if a significant quantity of methane were to be freed into the atmosphere, the resulting contribution to global warming could be cataclysmic. Is there enough methane trapped in hydrates to make much of a difference in this regard? There is, and by a long shot. Altogether, there is roughly 3,000 times more methane locked up as hydrates than is currently found in Earth's atmosphere. Even without attempts at commercial exploitation, oceanic hydrates are already responsible for between 5 and 10 million tons of methane emissions to the atmosphere each year.

Seabed methane hydrates already represent a serious environmental threat in the context of global-warming trends. As the temperature of the oceans rises, hydrate deposits may become unstable. This could release large amounts of methane into the atmosphere, thus greatly exacerbating the greenhouse effect, which would in turn warm the oceans even further. The result could be a self-reinforcing feedback loop with unimaginably horrific consequences.

Adding commercial extraction procedures to this existing precarious situation hardly seems prudent. Some scientists, including Charles Paull, a researcher with the Monterey Bay Aquarium, say that extracting gas hydrates could disrupt seafloor stability.[1] Geologists suspect that the large-scale breakdown of methane hydrate deposits was responsible for huge underwater landslips and the creation of massive tsunami waves earlier in Earth's history, as well as for sudden periods of intense global warming. If in the future unstable hydrates were dislodged by attempts to extract them, the result could be a modern rerun of those ancient cataclysms, with immense waves sloshing across the oceans, scouring the surfaces of islands and inundating coastal cities, while the entire planet baked under a methane fog.

Nonetheless, when the human economic need is great enough, we can be sure that attempts will be made to produce usable energy from methane hydrates. Resource-poor Japan (which imports nearly all of its oil and gas) is already involved in research in hydrate beds along the Nankai Trough, some 3,500 feet (1,100 meters) under water, and at an international test site in the frozen Mackenzie River delta in northern Canada. In 2002, the Japan National Oil Corporation announced some success in the Mackenzie Delta tests. Japan hopes to determine by 2011 whether commercial methane hydrate mining is feasible; if it is, efforts could begin by 2015.

In the US, Congress has appropriated $47 million for methane hydrate research over the next few years — though many of the funded projects are mostly academic, with methane deposits on the moons of Jupiter and Saturn envisioned as a fuel source for future space travel. However, as the North American natural gas crisis deepens, there will be increasing incentive to explore the possibility of extracting methane from coastal seabeds or frozen tundras. The US Geological Survey has estimated that the quantity of gas hydrates in the United States is equal to roughly 200 times the conventional natural gas resources remaining in the country; according to the Department of Energy, if only one percent of the deposits could be exploited for domestic consumption, the US could more than double its supply of energy resources.

The exploitation of land-based methane hydrates is especially likely to garner increasing interest — but the technical hurdles in this instance are almost as problematic as in the case of seabed deposits. Russian engineers have suggested pumping nuclear waste under the Siberian permafrost to thaw the hydrate fields there so that they can be exploited. Such methods are sure to provoke quite an outcry from environmentalists and native populations if applied in North America.

Will methane hydrates be the energy source of the future? Don't hold your breath. The inevitable efforts in that direction may or may not yield useful net energy; in either case, intense battles will be waged between environmentalists on one hand and government and industry leaders on the other. The stakes will be breathtaking: if the concerns of Earth scientists are well founded, and if a miscalculation were to occur, the damage could be incalculable. With the development of the hydrogen bomb, humanity was forced to confront the fact that it had invented a means for its own extinction. If an industry emerges devoted to seabed methane hydrate extraction, humankind might find itself facing another similarly stark awakening.

High on Hydrogen

These days it seems that everyone is abuzz about hydrogen. For politicians, the promotion of a hydrogen economy seems to be a litmus requirement for "green" credentials. President Bush has promised $1.2 billion for research into a hydrogen-powered "freedom" car, while California governor Arnold Schwarzenegger has proposed "hydrogen highways" with H_2 filling stations every 20 miles. And the US Department of Energy has made between $1 million and $3.5 million available to "provide support for activities intended to educate key target audiences, including teachers, students, and the public about the use of hydrogen as an energy carrier and the future path to a hydrogen economy."[2]

My own assessment of hydrogen's potential to shape our energy future is critical and cautious. I believe that there will be important niche applications in which hydrogen will prove to be a useful energy storage medium and an efficiency strategy (for example, a former student of mine at New College has built a small hydrogen device that he claims improves the fuel efficiency of his truck). But the idea of a full-blown "hydrogen economy" is probably more hype than reality.

I say this with some regret, as many hydrogen advocates are people whose motives I respect. I am thinking now of Jeremy Rifkin, whose 2002 book *The Hydrogen Economy* covered much of the same material in its first few chapters, as *The Party's Over* does (my manuscript was already with the publisher when *The Hydrogen Economy* was released).[3] I learned much from Rifkin's previous books, and I greatly respect his pioneering critical work on the subject of genetic engineering. However, it seemed to me that the last two chapters of his book — which describe a relatively easy transition to a utopian future of distributed energy production from renewable sources mediated by hydrogen — are not well thought-through.

Rifkin's enthusiasm for hydrogen seems to be based at least partly on the work of Amory Lovins of the Rocky Mountain Institute (RMI). Lovins is another person I respect a great deal: he has been promoting energy conservation and renewable energy sources since the 1970s with intelligence and ingenuity. In the past few years, Lovins has written a great deal about hydrogen, and the RMI web site features over two hundred articles touting fuel cells and the ultra-efficient "hypercar" that he and his colleagues propose as a replacement for Americans' present overweight, petroleum-fed, internal-combustion monsters.

However, over the past year or so a few authoritative technical studies have raised serious questions about hydrogen's efficiency and environmental safety. A paper titled "The Future of the Hydrogen

Economy: Bright or Bleak," by fuel cell consultant Ulf Bossel and Baldur Eliasson of ABB Switzerland Ltd., published in January 2003, concluded that the physical and chemical properties of hydrogen make it unsuitable as an energy carrier, and that new technological developments are unlikely to change this assessment. The two scientists studied hypothetical schemes for the manufacture, transportation, storage, and use of hydrogen *as whole systems*, and found that:

> an elemental "Hydrogen Economy" for road transport would have a low well-to-tank efficiency and hence a low environmental quality. In particular, if the electrical energy were generated in coal-fired power plants, the well-to-tank efficiency might fall below 20 percent. Even if the hydrogen were used in fuel cells, the overall energy efficiency would be comparable to that of steam engines in the early half of the 20th century, while the CO_2 emissions would have significantly increased due to the growth of overall energy consumption.[4]

A paper published in *Science* (July 18, 2003) by Alex Farrell, assistant professor of energy and resources at UC Berkeley, and David Keith, associate professor of engineering and public policy, reached similar conclusions. Farrell and Keith discussed various short- and long-term strategies they say would achieve the efficiency benefits claimed for hydrogen cars — but at a fraction of the cost. "Hydrogen cars are a poor short-term strategy, and it's not even clear that they are a good idea in the long term," Farrell told reporter Robert Sanders in a subsequent interview.[5]

The scientists found that technically simple (but politically dicey) improvements to current cars and current environmental rules would be more than 100 times cheaper than a transition to hydrogen when it comes to reducing air pollution. Simply increasing fuel efficiency standards would achieve impressive benefits at a trivial cost. And if the goal is to reduce greenhouse gases, the best strategy would be to focus on carbon dioxide emissions from electric power plants.

Farrell speculates that hydrogen has received uncritical attention from across the political spectrum partly because "it doesn't challenge drivers to change their habits. It also doesn't challenge the auto industry to change its behavior, providing, instead, a subsidy for research that will lead to better cars whether they are hydrogen-powered or gasoline-powered."[6]

Meanwhile, a study at the California Institute of Technology in Pasadena led by Los Alamos National Laboratory scientist Yuk Yung has found that hydrogen — which is typically described as being "non-polluting" — may have hidden costs. Because it is so light and its molecules are so small, hydrogen will inevitably leak from storage containers and pipelines. As the escaped hydrogen rises through the atmosphere, it will react with oxygen to form water. In tiny quantities, this would hardly be a problem. But if humankind were truly to develop a "hydrogen economy," the quantities released could be enough to make the stratosphere wetter, which would in turn cool the lower stratosphere, particularly in the polar regions. The end result would be a further disruption of the ozone layer that protects the Earth's surface from harmful ultraviolet light.[7]

On the other hand, there are positive recent developments regarding hydrogen. For example, various researchers have found more efficient ways to make hydrogen from fossil fuels by replacing the expensive precious metals used today with much cheaper materials.[8] And a company called the Renewable Energy Corporation (RECO) has apparently developed a method to harness and concentrate the power of the sun, using a system of mirrors, to crack water molecules, thereby releasing the hydrogen. The process bypasses electrical generation and makes hydrogen directly, thus increasing efficiency dramatically.[9]

However, these efforts address only some of hydrogen's problems. Briefly, the remaining arguments *against* hydrogen can be summarized as follows:

1. Hydrogen is not a source of energy, just a way of storing it. Hydrogen must be made from coal, oil, natural gas, wood,

soft biomass, electricity, or — according to RECO promotional literature — water and sunlight. In the future, as oil and natural gas become scarce, existing fuels will be essential for other needs. It is as yet unclear whether the RECO process will be scalable, or if it will live up to its advertised advantages.

2. Spending money on hydrogen takes away investment from primary sources such as wind and solar — as well as from highly marginal current sources such as wave and tidal generators, which are beginning to show some promise.

3. Most of the advantages of hydrogen depend on the vaunted efficiency of fuel cells. But when the inefficiencies of converting other energy into hydrogen are taken into account, these efficiencies nearly disappear. Moreover, the cost of fuel cells — which have been around for decades — is still very high.

4. The coal and nuclear industries look favorably on hydrogen because the demand for electricity to produce it will inevitably increase (unless all hydrogen is made from natural gas or coal — and natural gas seems like a dubious bet, as we saw in Chapter 1). With nuclear- and coal-based electricity being used to produce hydrogen, these industries could describe themselves as producers of clean, non-polluting energy (though see the California Institute of Technology study above). Yet even if the conversion process were efficient, it would still be next-to-impossible to build enough new generating plants to satisfy America's transportation needs. And the other downsides of coal and nuclear power plants are well known: coal is polluting, and mining it is ecologically ruinous; with nuclear power, the present generation enjoys the benefit while the next generation pays for cleanup costs.

5. The storage and transportation of hydrogen are largely unsolved problems. Storage tanks have been developed, but they are large and prohibitively expensive as compared to conventional automotive gasoline tanks. Compressing or liquefying hydrogen takes energy, only some of which can be

recovered later. Piping hydrogen is also a problem because of the energy required for pumping: the gas's low volumetric energy density results in a need for higher flow rates, which in turn leads to greater flow resistance. As a result, it takes about 4.6 times more energy to move hydrogen through a pipeline than is the case for natural gas. Moreover, hydrogen is not compatible with the current natural gas piping infrastructure due to the brittleness of materials, inadequacy of seals, and the incompatibility of pump lubrication.

6. We need a solution now, not decades from now. In replacing dwindling fossil fuels we can achieve faster results by improving present cars, raising efficiency standards, and redesigning our economy to reduce the need for long-distance transport, than we can by attempting a costly and uncertain transition to a hydrogen economy. These more prosaic steps would nevertheless be more politically difficult, because they would require decision makers to resist the lobbying of the powerful oil and automotive industries.

Again: hydrogen may have a range of useful functions in a post-petroleum economy. But more studies need to be done on its practicality *before* large sums are invested in new infrastructure. At this point, much of the enthusiasm about hydrogen seems to be issuing from politics rather than science.

Why Even the Perfect Energy Source Will Not Sustain Growth Indefinitely

Whether or not hydrogen plays a significant role in our energy future, we will almost certainly continue to rely overwhelmingly on primary sources of energy with which we are already familiar — including the sun, wind, nuclear power, and coal. But as supplies of oil and natural gas are depleted, the mix of fuels and sources on which we depend will inevitably shift.

In Chapter 4 of *The Party's Over*, after discussing the various alternatives to oil, I concluded that no single candidate, or likely mix, would be capable of supplying industrial societies with the quantity and quality of energy necessary to sustain economic growth into the middle decades of the current century, and that the consequences will likely be serious, if not catastrophic.

Since the publication of that book, many other alternative energy sources have presented themselves. No doubt many of these have merit. If the RECO hydrogen generation system described above works as claimed, it would certainly assist in the post-petroleum energy transition, even if industrial societies do not develop fully-fledged hydrogen economies for a range of reasons. Many of my readers have asked if I've heard of thermal depolymerization — a recycling process that promises to produce synthetic oil from a variety of organic materials. The process was discussed in glowing terms in an article ("Anything into Oil") in the April, 2003 issue of *Discover* magazine. Since *Discover* is an organ of the corporate press and not a peer-reviewed journal, we will have to wait and see if thermal depolymerization can actually deliver on the promises made in that article. If so, it could assist in increasing the energy efficiency of modern societies. Still another energy alternative is a tidal system being developed by a Canadian company called Blue Energy, in which "Multiple vertical axis Davis Hydro Turbines are mounted in a modular duct structure to form a tidal fence or tidal bridge, across a river, tidal estuary or ocean channel." According to the company's website, "The Blue Energy Power System is expected to be one of the cheapest energy sources on the planet within the next decade."[10] Again, time will tell. And just recently, STMicroelectronics, Europe's largest semiconductor maker, said that it has found a way to make a new type of photovoltaic solar cell using cheap organic materials such as plastics to bring down their price dramatically, enough to make PV electricity competitive with electricity generated using natural gas.[11]

Several readers have also touted various "free-energy" machines — of which I tend to be more skeptical. I admit that my doubts are based not on an actual examination of the machines in question, but only on a grasp of general physical principles.

It is difficult to say which of these various alternatives holds the most promise, especially given the fact that most of the information we have about them comes from manufacturers or promoters who have an interest in emphasizing the cheapness or practicality of their products. We desperately need a way to sort out the complicated technical issues surrounding society's choice of energy alternatives. This should be the purpose of an ongoing, expert, unbiased (to the degree that is possible) commission whose job it is to evaluate all available energy alternatives across a range of transparent criteria. Those criteria would include energy profit ratios, environmental impacts, scalability, renewability, and convenience of use. Tests would need to be repeated periodically because of the introduction of new technologies and the depletion of resources (for example, the energy profit ratio from prospecting for and extracting natural gas in a given region may be very different in five years from what it is today). In addition, the commission should be open to testing unusual energy sources and high-efficiency engines — including "free-energy" machines. If there is merit to such devices, the world would soon know; on the other hand, scam artists would quickly be exposed.

One might think that this should be the business of the International Energy Agency or the US Department of Energy. But these bodies haven't seen fit to undertake the task, obvious and profound as the need may be. Currently, I am in discussion with several independent energy analysts about creating a citizens' energy alternatives evaluation commission via a nonprofit organization — the Post Carbon Institute.[12] The effort can succeed only if we are able to coordinate the volunteer efforts of dozens of energy experts around the world via the Internet. Our project is currently only in the early planning stages.

On the basis of current knowledge, I would guess that there probably is a transition strategy, based on the available alternative energy sources, that could in theory, with great effort and considerable sacrifice on the part of the general population, produce as much energy as industrial societies actually need in order to supply the basic necessities of life to their current populations, at least for the next couple of decades (please note that I am *not* saying that there could be sufficient resources to supply a growing population within a growing economy). If such a strategy were identified and implemented, would that mean that the problem raised by our dependence on oil and natural gas has been solved? Not necessarily. Even in the best imaginable case — let us suppose for the moment that one of the many free-energy devices currently being peddled actually turns out to work, and that industrial societies' energy appetites can be fully satisfied for the foreseeable future — we still face an immense difficulty. I discussed this at the end of Chapter 1, but because many people may find the point difficult to grasp, I return to it now.

Our real problem is that we are trapped in a perpetual growth machine. As long as modern societies need economic growth in order to stave off collapse (as is clearly the case today, given existing debt-and-interest-based national currencies), we will continue to require ever more resources on a yearly basis from our already overtaxed earthly environment. But the Earth has limited resources; even renewable resources like trees and rainfall are replenished only at a certain rate. Moreover, some of us humans (particularly those of us who live in rich, industrialized countries) want a lot more than basic necessities. We have become accustomed to a high standard of living — indeed, to an unsustainably high standard — and we wish that standard to be available to a *constantly growing population*.

The energy conundrum is thus intimately tied to the fact that we anticipate perpetual growth within a finite system. We developed this expectation during the recent historical period in which vast supplies of nonrenewable energy resources became available, and we understandably (though foolishly) came to believe that the party would never end.

Thus, our predicament is not entirely reducible to the fact that we are now starting to run out of the cheap energy sources on which we have become dependent. That is, in my view, the *aspect* of the predicament that is most likely to present itself to us first and most forcibly, but the predicament itself is broader and deeper. In essence, the crisis we face is — again, as discussed in Chapter 1 — essentially a particularly nasty instance of the universal ecological dilemma of population pressure, resource depletion, and habitat destruction.

We humans recently discovered a strategy for defeating population pressure by extracting fossil energy resources and burning them in machines that in turn enabled us to intensify our extraction and use of other resources (water, topsoil, fish, minerals, trees, etc.). Through the application of this strategy, we have conquered virtually every ecosystem and increased our numbers dramatically. We have, at least temporarily, increased the human carrying capacity of our environment by hundreds of percent. But avoiding population pressure has predictably resulted in resource depletion and habitat disruption. While short-term carrying capacity has doubled, redoubled, and doubled yet again, it appears that we are in fact degrading the long-term carrying capacity of our environment to a level far below its status at the time we began the exercise. Will finding a supply-side solution in the form of the perfect energy resource (once more, let us hypothesize the possibility of free energy), without dealing head-on with the universal ecological dilemma, enable us to continue in the pattern of life we have come to accept as "normal"?

There are many economists and techno-optimists who believe that it can. After all, more energy could generate substitutes for other resources. For example, if we had enough energy available we could make up for shortages in fresh water by desalinizing ocean water in vast quantities. The oceans may be running out of stocks of wild fish, but with enough available cheap energy we could simply farm as many fish as we needed. Eventually, using biotechnology and nanotechnology, we should be able to synthesize any substance we desired. Even if wild nature disappears altogether, this should present no obstacle. We could create artificial environments of any kind we chose — so long as we had enough energy. Running out of metals? No problem! Get them from Mars. Too many people? No problem! Put them on space ships and establish colonies on other planets.

There is no way to fully disconfirm this cheery vision of what people could accomplish, given unlimited power — without actually running the experiment. But we will be able to run the experiment only once if at all (remember: currently it is by no means clear that a free-energy source exists). Since the entire Earth is the proposed laboratory and the experiment would be irreversible, one can perhaps be forgiven for feeling a momentary flush of squeamish caution.

In principle, however, we have already run the "free-energy" experiment, on a smaller scale, several times in human history, and other species have run it as well. Every time we humans have found a way to harvest a dramatically increased amount of food or fuel from the environment, we have been presented with a quantity of energy that is, if not entirely free, at least cheap and abundant relative to what we had previously. Each time, we have responded by increasing our population, and correspondingly, the load on the environmental systems that sustain us. Each time, we have ended up degrading the environment and creating the conditions for a crash. When we first migrated from Africa tens of thousands of years ago and discovered new continents then filled with edible megafauna — mastodons, mammoths, giant sloths, and so on — we found what seemed to be an inexhaustible protein source. We continued our migrations, expanding our population and killing large animals as we went. Evidence suggests that we hunted many of these species to extinction, and the resulting collapse in our food supply meant that we had to adjust to eating smaller game and cultivated plants. Agriculture gave us another energy boost, but one agricultural civilization after another — from that of the Mesopotamians to that of the Mayans — built densely populated cities and high cultures, and then collapsed after exhausting the soil and cutting too many trees.

The same pattern plays out with other species whenever they discover a significant temporary food subsidy. The behavior has been observed so many times, in so many species and human societies, that it really has to be considered a standard response. The Industrial Revolution was our most recent and dramatic human experience with "free" energy (in the forms of coal, oil, and natural gas), and these fuels have proven to be a windfall of unbelievable proportions. In Texas in the 1930s, oil was literally cheaper than drinking water — and it still is, if we're talking about the water in one-pint containers sold at convenience stores. What have we done with this windfall? We have increased our population from 800 million to 6.4 billion in a little over three centuries and brought the planet to the verge of ecological ruin. This should come as no surprise. Any other species would have done essentially the same.

So if some new free-energy device were to become available tomorrow, how would people respond? We really don't need to speculate much. Absent a self-limiting, culturally reinforced Powerdown program, we can be virtually 100 percent sure that the response would be to continue population growth, and to increase the harvesting of other resources from the environment, until Liebig's Law got us in one way or another.

Liebig's Law, named after the 19th century German soil scientist Justus von Liebig, is sometimes called the Law of the Minimum. It tells us that the carrying capacity for any given species is set by the necessity in least supply. Every species has a list of requirements for survival — water, temperature range, degree of salinity of water, degree of acidity or alkalinity of soil, food of a certain nature, so many hours of sunlight, and so on. Liebig's Law tells us that even if all other factors are optimal, the lack of one necessity can undermine an organism's ability to survive.

This puts a tough burden on humans' attempts to completely manage a fully artificial environment. We might get nearly everything perfect (plenty of fresh water, enough proteins and carbohydrates, enough oxygen), and yet fail to adequately manage *just one* factor, and the result would be catastrophic. The failure of the Biosphere experiments — in which highly equipped and well-prepared scientists attempted to establish an artificial, fully enclosed, self-sustaining environment — is a case in point.

In my own mind, an understanding of Liebig's Law inspires a profound respect for wild nature. Somehow, through endless mutual accommodations over hundreds of millions of years, untold numbers of species have managed to adjust themselves to their environments, and their environments to themselves, in such a way that they can mutually survive. Of course, none do so forever: a given species appears, flourishes for a few tens or hundreds of thousands of years, and then dies out as conditions change. In the meantime, a wondrous and delicate balance enables that species to cooperate with others in the maintenance of the web of existence.

Are we humans clever enough to replace that mutually woven and continually micro-adjusted network of interdependence with an artificial system of our own design that is capable of satisfying all of our basic needs well into the future? Again, some people may think so, but not, I'd guess, many people with much familiarity with how nature actually works. Yes, we need energy. And, ultimately, energy is everything — in the sense that life and matter are themselves reducible to energy. But we humans are biological creatures that have evolved in the context of complex ecosystems. We depend on the services of thousands of other species for our survival. If we seriously upset the systems on which we depend, we will most likely merely reconfirm the universality of the Law of the Minimum and the inevitability of the ecological dilemma.

Of course we wish to find a way to preserve our current way of life. No one wants to undertake basic change unless we have to, especially if doing so means restrictions on reproduction and individual consumption. But, as I have said already, business as usual is not an option, even if there is a solution to the energy problem in isolation. The oil-depletion crisis is merely the current mask for the timeless ecological dilemma. The way out of that dilemma requires no technological breakthrough; indeed, purely technical "solutions" may only distract us from addressing the underlying problem.

The way out is to restrict per-capita resource usage and to reduce the human population. If we take the Powerdown path, then alternative energy sources could help. If we refuse to power down, then *nothing* will help.

In the end, self-limitation is the only answer that counts, but that is the answer that no one wants to hear. So we sit, and wait, and assume, and deny. And as we wait, the signs of depletion worsen and global resource wars loom. If we refuse to take the hard Powerdown path, after a while we will simply have no choice: we will compete for what is left (whether for oil, natural gas, water, or phosphates) or we will die. Plan Snooze simply leads us back to Plan War.

CHAPTER FIVE

Building Lifeboats

The Path of Community Solidarity and Preservation

"My name is Ozymandias, king of kings:
Look on my works, ye Mighty, and despair!"
Nothing beside remains. Round the decay
Of that colossal wreck, boundless and bare
The lone and level sands stretch far away.

— *Ozymandias*, Percy Bysshe Shelley

Things that can't go on forever don't.

—Herbert Stein, chairman of the Council of
Economic Advisers during the Nixon administration

If the aim of the Last One Standing strategy is to shift the pain of resource depletion from the most militarily powerful countries onto others less formidable so that an affluent industrial lifestyle can be preserved for at least a few people; if the aim of Plan Powerdown is to avert collapse globally by voluntarily cutting back on levels of population and resource consumption; then Plan Snooze merely hopes that the problem, if ignored, will take care of itself. Of these strategies, only Powerdown appears likely to be effective in the long run. Yet for any national leader — or, at least, any prominent US politician — to publicly advocate it would be political suicide. Should we not therefore permit ourselves to think the unthinkable?

Perhaps, as I have indicated already, the collapse of industrial societies is at this point unavoidable. Still more distressing is the likelihood that the collapse will not occur in a measured, controlled manner. The managers in charge of the world's economic, political, and military regimes are immensely powerful within the context of the present world system, but they may be utterly incapable of preventing the disintegration of that system, since the only actions they can take that will be significantly effective toward that end will also tend to undermine their own power and authority vis-à-vis competing regimes and managers. Thus, the system actively discourages steps toward its own preservation.

That is indeed a bitter pill to swallow. It takes more than a few minutes to come to terms with the implications. Perhaps for the moment it may be better just to consider collapse as a possibility, a mere hypothesis. *If this is what is in store, what should our response be?*

Our first instinctual thought must inevitably travel along the lines of personal and family survival. Where should we go? What would we need? What sort of climate, how much garden space? What would be our water source? Should we stock up on guns and ammo?

It doesn't take long, following that path, to arrive at a dead end. It is difficult to plan for personal survival in the context of unpredictable social chaos. If I have a garden but my neighbors are hungry, I must either defend my land with deadly force or watch my crops disappear. But what if someone else has more guns, or comes when I am asleep?

Ultimately, personal survival will depend on community survival. But, then, if my community is prospering while neighboring communities are mired in hunger and violence, then my community will have to defend itself. And if my community does manage to preserve itself, what will life be like after the disappearance of communication networks (including television, radio, newspapers, and book publishers), the collapse of school systems and libraries — in short, the vanishing of the entire cultural infrastructure that enables us to understand our world and communicate across time and space?

Might human cultural life descend to mere existence? Pre-industrial peoples at least had elaborate oral traditions that grounded their communities in the local terrain and wove together the needs and interests of generations. The industrial interval has shredded traditional cultures and replaced them with a global consumer spectacle. Once the latter is gone, the survivors of its demise will run the risk of becoming cultureless wraiths condemned to subsist on decaying memories of what life was like before the great crash, but with few living traditions to guide them.

Thus, as industrial civilization sputters and dies, it will make sense for us to try to preserve as much as possible both of nature and of whatever practical knowledge, music, art, or philosophy can help sustain us and our descendants.

In this chapter we will peer into the abyss. What might collapse look like? Who has the best chance to survive? And how can we best prepare ourselves?

How Civilizations Collapse

Even though many previous civilizations have fallen, history can give us only a general idea of what to expect as our own comes apart at the seams. Nevertheless, it is worth taking a few moments to glean what we can in this regard.

I cited Joseph Tainter's book *The Collapse of Complex Societies* at some length in Chapter 1 of *The Party's Over;* for the past decade-and-a-half his work has been widely regarded as the best treatment of the subject in print. However, an unpublished paper by John Michael Greer raises the study of collapse to a new level.[1]

According to Greer, when societies enter an expansion phase without effective limits to growth, the process tends to become self-reinforcing. Using historical examples, Greer identifies the conditions under which societies that have entered a growth phase are more likely to approach a steady state, or to descend into one of two forms of collapse — a *maintenance crisis* or a *depletion crisis*. A society that uses resources at or below replenishment rate is more likely to experience a maintenance crisis; in this case, production of new capital falls short of maintenance needs; "capital of all kinds cannot be maintained and is converted to waste: physical capital is destroyed or spoiled, human populations decline in number, large-scale social organizations disintegrate into smaller and more economical forms, and information is lost." Greer cites the example of imperial China from the tenth century B.C.E. to the end of the 19th century C.E., where:

> Efficient cereal agriculture and local market economies provided the foundation for a series of [growth] cycles resulting in the establishment of centralized imperial dynastic states. These [growth] cycles drove increases in population, public works such as canals and flood control projects, and sociopolitical organization, which proved unsustainable over the long term. As maintenance costs exceeded the imperial government's resources, repeated maintenance crises led to the breakup of national unity, invasion by neighboring peoples, loss of infrastructure and steep declines in population.

A society that uses resources beyond replenishment rate is more likely to undergo a depletion crisis, in which the key features of a maintenance crisis are exacerbated by the depletion of resources essential for production. The collapse of the western Roman Empire, according to Greer, was an example of a destructive, self-consuming collapse driven by combined maintenance and resource crises. Greer continues:

> While the ancient Mediterranean world, like imperial China, was primarily dependent on readily replenished resources, the Empire itself was the product of a [growth] cycle fueled by easily depleted resources and driven by Roman military superiority. Beginning in the

third century B.C.E., Roman expansion transformed the capital of other societies into resources for Rome, as country after country was conquered and stripped of movable wealth. Each new conquest increased the Roman resource base and helped pay for further conquests. After the first century C.E., though, further expansion failed to pay its own costs. All remaining states within the reach of Rome were either barbarian states with little wealth, such as the Germans, or rival empires capable of defending themselves, such as the Parthians. Without income from new conquests, the maintenance costs of empire proved unsustainable, and a [collapse] cycle followed rapidly. The first major breakdown in the imperial system came in 166 C.E., and further crises followed until the empire ceased to exist in 476 C.E.

Greer provides a rational scheme for understanding the causes and tempo of collapse in past societies, and, by implication, in our current one. However, before we proceed to unpack those implications further, let us examine the Roman collapse in more detail, and contrast it with that of the Classic Mayan civilization — which typifies a depletion-led collapse more starkly.

❖ ❖ ❖

Books have been written about the fall of Rome, and still there is controversy about the ultimate cause. However, there is a growing consensus that ecological factors played a significant part. From 58 B.C.E., Rome had guaranteed every citizen a daily ration of bread; but to produce enough grain to fulfill this promise, forests had to be cleared around much of the Mediterranean. Deforestation led to erosion and localized climate change, which in turn eventually forced the Romans to virtually abandon major cities in food-producing regions. As the Empire contracted, hostile tribes on the periphery moved in. However, there were also important military, economic, and political dimensions to these events. Tainter describes the matter this way:

As a solar-energy based society which taxed heavily, the empire had little fiscal reserve. When confronted with military crises, Roman Emperors often had to respond by debasing the silver currency . . . and trying to raise new funds. In the third century A.D. constant crises forced the emperors to double the size of the army and increase both the size and complexity of the government. To pay for this, masses of worthless coins were produced, supplies were commandeered from peasants, and the level of taxation was made even more oppressive (up to two-thirds of the net yield after payment of rent). Inflation devastated the economy. Lands and population were surveyed across the empire and assessed for taxes. Communities were held corporately liable for any unpaid amounts. While peasants went hungry or sold their children into slavery, massive fortifications were built, the size of the bureaucracy doubled, provincial administration was made more complex, large subsidies in gold were paid to Germanic tribes, and new imperial cities and courts were established. With rising taxes, marginal lands were abandoned and population declined. Peasants could no longer support large families. To avoid oppressive civic obligations, the wealthy fled from cities to establish self-sufficient rural estates. Ultimately, to escape taxation, peasants voluntarily entered into feudal relationships with these land holders. A few wealthy families came to own much of the land in the western empire, and were able to defy the imperial government. The empire came to sustain itself by consuming its capital resources. . . .[2]

Rome wasn't built in a day, nor did it fall instantly. The first signs of decline appeared as early as 161 C.E., during the reign of Marcus Aurelius, when invaders attacked from the east and north and a plague killed a quarter of the city's population. As time went on, class conflicts and political infighting took their toll, and the leadership foolishly assumed that they could rule by military might alone, when negotiation with the barbarian tribes was increasingly called for. Consequently, barbarians sacked the city and spread themselves throughout the western Mediterranean. Emperor Diocletian split the Empire into two geographically removed bureaucracies with two separate emperors and armies. He also battled inflation by freezing prices, and banned Christianity, which he blamed for Rome's problems. Constantine took a different approach, adopting Christianity and using it as a unifying force for the Roman people. He also moved the capital of the empire from Rome to Constantinople. This marked a political, cultural, and economic shift of the center of power to the Balkans, where important battlefronts still raged, instead of the West, which was by now overrun with barbarians.

Thus the "fall of Rome" actually consisted of many decades of decay punctuated by several relatively brief periods of invasion, plague, and rebellion. Between 400 and 800, the population of the city fell by roughly 90 percent. After the collapse, life went on, but in a very different way. What remained of Roman civilization and culture was now decentralized and selectively preserved by the Church in its widely scattered monasteries.

❖ ❖ ❖

During the centuries when Rome was in decline, the Mayan civilization of the Yucatan peninsula of Central America was at its height. This society, at its apex, was the most advanced in the Americas. The Maya had to rely on wells and reservoirs for drinking and irrigation through the dry season.

The Maya did not have the advantage of the food production methods used by the Romans — field agriculture based on plows pulled by draft animals. Rather, they relied on swidden, or slash-and-burn, horticulture. Corn supplied two-thirds of the Mayan diet. This food regime yielded only modest surpluses to support a social structure — which may explain why Mayan kingdoms never became unified, but remained isolated and continually competed with one another. The typical kingdom had a population of only about 50,000, and its territory extended a mere two days' walk from the capital. Jared Diamond, in his essay titled "The Last Americans," describes the political structure of the kingdoms this way:

> Presiding over the temple was the king himself, who functioned both as head priest and as political leader. It was his responsibility to pray to the gods, to perform astronomical and calendrical rituals, to ensure the timely arrival of the rains on which agriculture depended, and thereby to bring prosperity. The king claimed to have the supernatural power to deliver those good things because of his asserted family relationship to the gods. Of course, that exposed him to the risk that his subjects would become disillusioned if he couldn't fulfill his boast of being able to deliver rains and prosperity.[3]

Despite ecological limitations and political disunity, the Classic Maya nevertheless built a civilization that lasted 500 years, with a writing system, mathematics, astronomy, and a monumental architecture that rivaled and occasionally surpassed those of the Old World civilizations. The Classic period in Mayan history began around 250 C.E. From then, according to Diamond,

> . . . the Maya population increased almost exponentially, to reach peak numbers in the eighth century A.D. The largest monuments were erected toward the end of that century. All the indicators of a complex society declined throughout the ninth century, until the last date on any monument was A.D. 909. This decline of Maya population and architecture constitutes what is known as the Classic Maya collapse.

What happened? As the population grew, more land — often on hillsides — had to be put under cultivation. Forests were cut, resulting in increased erosion; this, along with the depletion of soil nutrients, resulted in decreasing yields. Recurrent droughts turned these simmering problems into crises. As Diamond points out, the unraveling was a complex process:

We can identify increasingly familiar strands in the Classic Maya collapse. One consisted of population growth outstripping available resources . . . . While population was increasing, the area of usable farmland paradoxically was decreasing from the effects of deforestation and hillside erosion.

The next strand consisted of increased fighting as more and more people fought over fewer resources. Maya warfare, already endemic, peaked just before the collapse. That is not surprising when one reflects that at least 5 million people, most of them farmers, were crammed into an area smaller than the state of Colorado. That's a high population by the standards of ancient farming societies, even if it wouldn't strike modern Manhattan-dwellers as crowded.

Bringing matters to a head was a drought that, although not the first one the Maya had been through, was the most severe . . . .

The final strand is political. Why did the kings and nobles not recognize and solve these problems? A major reason was that their attention was evidently focused on the short-term concerns of enriching themselves, waging wars, erecting monuments, competing with one another, and extracting enough food from the peasants to support all those activities.

As in Rome during its collapse, the population of the Mayan civilization declined — again by over 90 percent. The health of the survivors deteriorated too: studies of skeletons show increased signs of disease and malnutrition from about 650 C.E. on. Many Mayan institutions — including kingship and the Long Count calendars by which the kings had traced their descent many centuries back in time — disappeared as kingdom after kingdom fell into ruin. Nevertheless, other elements of Mayan culture survived — including

the spoken language as well as myths and some religious practices —
and are carried on today by the descendants of the people who built
the grand temples of Tikal and Palenque.

The consistencies between ancient Rome and the Classic Maya
continue across other cultures as well. In every instance, intensifica-
tion of food production sparked population growth and vice versa,
while both led to depletion of soil and other basic resources. In general, while civilizations seek to expand the short-term human carrying capacity of their environments, they actually tend to undercut its
long-term carrying capacity.

❖ ❖ ❖

Now perhaps we can draw some general conclusions about what
happens as complex societies disintegrate. Collapse is seldom instan-
taneous, and it can begin within decades of the apex of a civilization's power, geographic extent, and population. Complex societies
that are limited to a single bioregion, such as the Classic Maya or the
Anasazi, are more likely to collapse quickly as a result of damage to
the ecosystem, while those of greater geographic extent typically
persist for decades or centuries longer. Meanwhile, there can be periods of relative stability and even moderate improvements. And various regions may decline at sharply differing rates. As certain aspects
of the social edifice begin to crumble, transitional structures arise.
Incompetent leadership often plays a role in the process: the people
in charge don't take the appropriate action, because this would
require a dramatic change of policies; instead, they intensify existing
efforts, which usually only makes matters worse. Warfare follows
from increasing competition for diminishing resources. And finally,
population levels fall dramatically as a result of famine, disease, and
fighting.

Sometimes as one civilization weakens it is simply conquered by
another. If the civilization in question has arisen in isolation from
others and is therefore immune from outside takeover, its surviving
peoples may rebuild peasant societies that preserve some elements of
the former high culture. In still other instances, and especially if the

decline was due to a maintenance crisis rather than a depletion crisis, a new civilization may arise from the ashes of the old after a few decades or centuries.

These are the lessons of the past. However, we should also keep in mind the ways in which present circumstances differ from previous ones. Today's industrial society is the first *global* civilization in history. It is characterized by interlocking systems of trade such that hardly a single country today is entirely self-sufficient in food, energy, or other basic necessities. Its environmental impacts are global in extent, so that the survivors will not be able simply to move elsewhere in order to escape. Moreover, today's industrial civilization has developed weapons capable of extinguishing all higher life on the planet.

In the worst imaginable case, the collapse of our current civilization will be absolute and permanent: no one will survive. However, it is more likely that collapse will be survivable, at least for some.

Most significantly, because industrial civilization is drawing down important resources far more quickly than they can be replenished, its fall will almost certainly have the characteristics of a depletion-led collapse. According to Greer, if depletion is limited by decreased drawdown of resources as a consequence of diminished production, the crisis may play out much like a maintenance crisis. However, "a society in which depletion is advanced . . . may not be able to escape catabolic collapse even if such steps are taken. Cultural and political factors may also make efforts to avoid catabolic collapse difficult to accomplish, or indeed to contemplate."[4]

A possible scenario for the collapse of our own civilization might go something like this: Energy shortages commence in the second decade of the century, leading to economic turmoil, frequent and lengthening power blackouts, and general chaos. Over the course of several years, food production plummets, resulting in widespread famine, even in formerly wealthy countries. Wars — including civil wars — rage intermittently. Meanwhile ecological crisis also tears at the social fabric, with water shortages, rising sea levels, and severe storms wreaking further havoc. While previous episodic disasters could have been dealt with by disaster management and rescue efforts, by now societies are too disorganized to mount such efforts. One after another, central governments collapse. Societies attempt to shed complexity in stages, thus buying time. Empires devolve into nations; nations into smaller regional or tribal states. But each lower stage — while initially appearing to offer a new beginning and a platform of stability — reaches its own moment of unsustainability and further collapse ensues. Between 2020 and 2100, the global population declines steeply, perhaps to fewer than one billion. By the start of the next century, the survivors' grandchildren are entertained by stories of a great civilization of the recent past in which people flew in metal birds and got everything they wanted by pressing buttons.

Who Will Survive?

Some places will probably be more hospitable than others following the crash. One wouldn't want to be in a region where massive energy inputs are required for heating or cooling. Neither would one wish to be in a region in which everyone is armed to the teeth, or one that is teeming with people. On the whole, countries where the population is already living with few energy inputs will probably be better off than those where per-capita energy usage is high. Indigenous people who have not lost their life-sustaining traditions may do well, if they live in places that have few covetable natural resources. However, the number of relatively undisturbed indigenous societies is dwindling year by year. And global climate change will challenge the survival skills of even the most tenacious tribes.

But suppose one is living in a fairly densely populated industrial nation and has no intention of moving. Then the discussion turns to the question, who within that society will have the highest probability of survival, and why?

At first thought, it might seem that the richest and most powerful people would have the best chance of weathering the events of the coming century. With enough money, they could buy a hilltop fortress, or erect security fences, or build private solar power stations, or hire guards and gardeners, or do a hundred other things to maintain themselves. This reasoning is sound up to a point: wealthy individuals could in fact become local warlords, the power holders in a feudal "Mad Max" society of the future.

However, wealth in and of itself will confer no guarantee of well-being. After a certain point, money is likely to lose value, and immediately useful goods will instead become the basis of trade. Moreover, many currently wealthy individuals are not equipped to do well as industrial civilization collapses: they are even more dependent than most other people on electronic gadgetry, long-distance travel, and a smoothly functioning social system. Imagine, for example, the plight of the well-off Manhattan stockbroker, or the Hong Kong currency trader, when lights go out and food shipments to local supermarkets are interrupted.

In North America, one group of people that is fairly well prepared to survive the disintegration of industrialism is the Amish. For American urbanites who know little about rural life it may seem perverse to hold up as a positive example a religious group that refuses to educate its children beyond the eighth grade, wears peculiar clothing, and eschews modern technology, but those who have rubbed elbows with the Amish will immediately appreciate the truth of what I am saying.

Also called the "Plain People," the Old Order Amish originated in Switzerland in the early sixteenth century as a division of the Mennonites or Anabaptists. They take their name from a Swiss Anabaptist, Jacob Amman, who taught the ethic of living a non-resistant life (the Amish do not serve in the military, but only in hospitals or alternate service), sharing material aid, living close to the soil, and following the Bible literally.

Bitterly victimized in Europe, the Amish were saved from extinction by William Penn, who granted them a haven from religious persecution in the New World. Since early colonial days, the Amish have preserved their distinctive culture, dress, language, and religion.

Today the Amish live in nineteen states, Canada, and Central America, though their numbers are highly concentrated in Pennsylvania, Ohio, and Indiana. They are immediately recognizable on the road or in town, the men wearing broad-brimmed hats and plain-cut trousers, the women and even little girls wearing bonnets and ankle-length dresses. They generally shun automobiles, airplanes, electricity, and telephones, and can be seen riding horse-drawn buggies on the rural gravel roads of most Midwestern states.

Amish pupils who have been given standardized tests by the US Office of Education usually perform above the norms of public school students in their communities. Amish young people, when they have reached adulthood, are given the opportunity either to stay with their community or to join the modern world, and most choose to stay. Amish customs are unquestionably restrictive, patriarchal, and quirky (unless you happen to agree with their version of Christianity), yet one has to admire the sheer persistence of a marginal cultural group that has been able to maintain what is essentially a 19th-century way of life well into the era of computers, cell phones, SUVs, hip-hop music, and action heroes.

If we were to single out the one factor that will best enable the Amish people to survive the end of industrial civilization while others perish, it would be their way of farming. Old Order Amish farmers use no tractors, chemical fertilizers, or chemical pesticides or herbicides. Moreover, their farming practices promote social cohesion: neighbors help each other during times of planting and harvest, and also join in barn raisings. Amish farmers minimize cash outlays for equipment and chemical inputs, and borrow as little as possible. As a result, most Amish farms are commercially successful, while other small American farms continue to go broke as a result of USDA and banking policies that favor corporate farms and giant agribusiness cartels.

A 25-year-old study on the productivity of Amish agriculture by W. A. Johnson, Victor Stoltzfus, and Peter Craumer ("Energy Conservation in Amish Argiculture," *Science*, Oct. 28, 1977) concluded that the Amish enjoy more moderate yields than conventional farmers. According to the authors of the study, Amish corn yields in Illinois ranged from 70 to 130 bushels per acre, while mechanized farmers reported 150–170 bushels. However, the Amish were able to more than make up for reduced productivity through savings on fuel, fertilizer, and equipment.

In his book *Amish Society,* John A. Hostetler quotes Amish farmers as saying that "tractors don't make manure" and "they ruin the land" by compacting soil. One Amishman told Hostetler that to buy an automobile would mean milking five more cows.[5] The Amish typically sell only enough produce to buy the things they cannot easily make for themselves. While the Amish are close to self-sufficiency, their labor-intensive way of life requires large families (these people may survive for the time being, but sooner or later they will have to learn the lesson currently being drilled into the deep psyche of all of humanity: restrict population growth or you will eventually suffer the consequences).

Will Amish communities and isolated native tribes survive while suburban American families starve? Perhaps. If so, the meek may inherit the Earth after all. In contemplating that possibility, we might feel justified in preaching the following Sermon on the Collapse:

> *Blessed are those who depend least on modern technology,*
> *for they have not forgotten how to take care of themselves.*
> *Blessed are those whose culture is communitarian and*
> *not individualist, for they will share and prosper.*
> *Blessed are they who have no exploitable natural*
> *resources, for no one will bother them.*
> *Blessed are those who know how to grow food, for they will*
> *eat and feed others.*

Yet I can't help wondering how helpful this is to the average reader. Can we all become Amish? How does one join up? Do we really have to wear those funny hats?

Saving What Is Best

In reality, no one can predict the exact pattern of the collapse, and there will probably be many different paths to survival. But that does not mean that strategizing is pointless. If we know that civilization is going down, we can do things to prepare. Moreover, we might seek to do better than merely to survive. After all, a worthwhile life is more than biological existence: we thrive on interactions with other humans in a complex context of language, meaning, and cultural expression. If much of that context were gone, life as such might be of little consequence. How might we go about planning for *cultural* survival?

As a scholar, my first impulse, when confronted with any important question, is to survey the literature. There is of course a flourishing survivalist genre, in which the books of Tom Brown Jr. (*The Tracker; Tom Brown's Field Guide to Wilderness Survival; Tom Brown's Field Guide to City and Suburban Survival;* etc.) hold a well-deserved position of prominence.[6] However, when it comes to published discussions of cultural survival in the context of the collapse of global industrial civilization, the pickings are rather slim.

One book that comes to mind is *The Coming Dark Age: What Will Happen When Modern Technology Breaks Down?*, by Roberto Vacca, published first in Italian in 1971, and in English in 1973.[7] Vacca's book caused quite a stir in the early 1970s, as oil prices soared during the Arab oil embargo, but it is scarcely remembered today. (His subsequent novel, *The Death of Megalopolis,* described in fictional terms the terrifying scenario of the downfall of the US.)[8]

Vacca's point was that "our great technological systems of human organization and association are continuously outgrowing ordered control: they are now reaching critical dimensions of instability." One could say that his thesis was disconfirmed, and that is why his book is largely forgotten: after all, the world did not end in 1975, nor in 1985, nor in 1995. Here we are, in the early years of the new millennium, and newspapers still arrive at our doorsteps each morning, the traffic signals still work, and everyone is busier than ever trying to avoid getting left behind by the accelerating pace of change. Since Vacca's book was written, the global human population has doubled, wars have been fought, and ecological crises have erupted, yet the ship of civilization is still afloat. The technological system has proved to be more resilient than he supposed. However, given what we now know about the approaching limits of global energy resources and global climate change, it is likely that Vacca was merely ahead of his time.

What can we glean from his warnings? The picture he paints of societal breakdown is predictably grim:

> In the imminent dark age people will endure hardship, and for the greater part of their time they will be laboring to satisfy primitive needs. A few — perhaps one in ten thousand — will have positions of privilege, and their work will not consist in battling personally against adversaries, or in cultivating the soil, or in building shelters with their own hands. It will consist in schemes and intrigues, grimmer and more violent than anything we know today, in order to maintain their personal privileges and to increase their personal power over others. Almost no one will be free from immediate burdens and able to think with detachment about abstract and general issues.[9]

In his last chapter, Vacca suggests a response:

> If in our day we foresee that a new medieval epoch is approaching, we shall not be able to save our souls without anticipating as best we can what measures be taken and what structures set up to save things in our civilization that we value most and to facilitate the efflorescence of a culture that, though certainly different from this one, may preserve at least certain of its characteristic traits — possibly the best.[10]

We need cultural preservation centers, says Vacca. Universities already perform some of this function, in his view, but colleges and universities are themselves in crisis. The groups of "conservers of civilization" that Vacca calls for share characteristics in common with "monastic fraternities" because they would necessarily be set apart from the outside world. After all, it was the monasteries of the medieval period that preserved the classics, the Latin language, and key Roman technologies, after the Empire itself crumbled. True, the religious fanaticism of some monks resulted in the destruction of many important classical texts, but it is doubtful if others would have survived without the monasteries — which served the combined functions of library, university, and research station.

THE PRIMITIVE TECHNOLOGY MOVEMENT

A decades-old grassroots movement to recreate and teach Paleolithic technologies offers an existing example of some features of a preservationist community. The primitive technology movement is not really a community per se, except in the virtual sense — members stay connected by way of e-mail, websites, newsletters, journals, and periodic gatherings. However, all movement members share a similar goal: the acquisition, preservation, and teaching of a range of practical skills that include flint knapping; hide tanning; the tracking, killing, and butchering of wild game; and the making of temporary shelters, skin clothing, stone tools, baskets, weirs, spears, bows, arrows, boomerangs, and other accoutrements of the Stone-Age lifestyle.

Modern science has learned much from primitive technologists: whereas archaeologists once had to conjecture (often quite inaccurately) about the uses of stone tools and the meanings of the piles of stone chips everywhere present at ancient camp sites, they now have practical knowledge on which to base their reconstructions of the past.

Primitive technologists tend to develop a profound respect for the natural world, and are practical conservationists. Some specialize in honing particular skills, or in leading wilderness training for young people.

This group's window into the past could offer guidance in the future: even if all of the survivors of the end of industrialism do not return to a Paleolithic pattern of existence, many will likely find themselves drawing on at least some of the practical skills preserved by the primitive technologists.

Primitive Technology home page:
<http://ic.net/~tbailey/Primitive.html>

Vacca makes some fairly detailed recommendations for how the preservationist "new monks" should get ready:

> The groups conserving civilized values and preparing for the renaissance will have to enjoy notable freedom from the immediate anxieties which would otherwise exhaust their energies; and this could happen only by means of an initial endowment made soon enough (that is, before the dark age actually begins) by the planners of the survival groups. This initial endowment could not be in money, since money will obviously be among the first of the various casualties when the systems break down. Instead, it would have to be an endowment of concrete things: tools, implements, motor-generator sets; nonperishable goods which a monastic community would make more of; goods exchangeable for food, particularly salt, sugar, and alcohol; drills, electric cells, copper wire, stainless steel screws, and small-arms ammunition.[11]

The "new monks" would need to conserve both abstract knowledge (for example, the details of human history) as well as understandings of how things are done — they would have to be skilled in the practical arts of the growing and preservation of food, metalworking, the keeping of animals, the making and use of hand tools, the making of clothing, the building of houses, as well as the building and operation of solar, wind, water, and biomass-powered energy systems with their attendant motors and energy storage technologies.

Of course, there is vastly more information about our current civilization that *could be* preserved than the "new monks" will have the capability of keeping. Moreover, increasing amounts of information (including musical and other recordings, images, and statistical data) are currently stored on electronic media. When electrical grids are no longer operational, much of this information will disappear, and most of the rest will become irretrievable. In addition, most existing books and magazines are printed on acid-bearing

paper that will disintegrate within decades. It seems likely, therefore, that most of the symbolic content of industrial societies will
vanish within a century or two, even if efforts are undertaken to
preserve it.

The "new monks" will therefore have to be highly selective,
continually deciding what information is worth keeping. The vast
majority of the information that is processed on a daily basis in
industrial societies — economic data, product advertising, and
political messages — is entirely dispensable anyway. It would be far
more important to keep scientific knowledge about how ecosystems
function, or about chemistry, physics, astronomy, geology, and
geography.

THE PRESERVATION OF LIFE

The genetic inheritance of cultivated food plant varieties is surely
among the most precious of humanity's treasures, and its preservation — past and present — is a fascinating subject for study. One
anecdote serves to highlight the profound importance of this field
of conservationist effort.

Russian scientist Nikolai I. Vavilov founded one of the first and
most important gene banks in the 1920s and '30s, following plant-
hunting trips in over 50 countries in Asia, the Americas, northern
Africa, and Europe, where he collected more than 50,000 seed
samples of wheat, rye, oats, peas, lentils, beans, chickpeas and
maize. By 1941, his collection included over 187,000 specimens,
and he had helped form a network of 400 research laboratories.

During the World War II Siege of Leningrad, Hitler's forces
shelled the city for over 7 months. When the siege began, institute
workers began growing out the most important specimens, fearing
they might be destroyed. They harvested underdeveloped potatoes
to save as seed and brought them to the institute's basement.
When winter came, there was little food and nothing with

In addition to practical skills, the survivors should seek to maintain certain aspects of social knowledge — the skills of small-group democratic decision-making, the principles of psychology, and historical and cross-cultural knowledge of world religions and the arts.

Given the immensity of the task, various groups would probably need to specialize in different areas of knowledge preservation. This specialization would probably occur automatically in any case, according to the unique interests of the individuals who devote themselves to the preservationist task.

Knowledge and tools are not all that will need keeping. The survivors will have to establish seed banks to preserve the genetic heritage from millennia of bioregionally-adapted agriculture. The

which to heat the Institute's remaining buildings. To keep the potatoes from freezing, workers burned boxes and paper. Though themselves half-frozen and starving, they guarded the precious specimens with their lives. When rumors spread through the bombed-out city that potatoes, rice, and other edible seeds were stored at the Institute, workers tightened security: no one was allowed to be alone inside any of the seed rooms. At least nine scientists and workers died from starvation rather than eat the seeds under their protection. Tragically, Vavilov himself had been arrested in 1940 and charged with espionage (due to false accusations by a scientific rival); he died in prison of malnutrition in 1943. The N. I. Vavilov All-Union Institute of Plant Industry, known worldwide by the abbreviation VIR, remains one of the most important gene banks in the world.

Today the world's genetic inheritance is diminishing rapidly — largely as a result of the merger and consolidation of seed companies and the globalization of industrial agriculture. Preservationist communities of the future will need to practice seed saving, and can be inspired by the example of Vavilov and his colleagues.

task of storing and growing out heirloom seeds must be undertaken immediately, as many varieties disappear forever each year, partly as a result of the economic consolidation of the global seed industry.

Perhaps the single most important thing to conserve for future generations would be the moral lesson inherent in the growth and collapse of industrial civilization. Nature is teaching us once again, this time in as dramatic a fashion as it is possible to imagine, that we must keep our population and per-capita drawdown of resources well within the regenerative capacity of our ecosystems. It is a simple lesson, but one that we seem apt to forget. If our descendants are fortunate, the memory of the fall of fossil-fuel-fed industrialism will become mythically ingrained in the collective psyche of our species, preventing the folly of temporary exuberance from reasserting itself — at least for a few millennia. But this will happen only if the collapse is correctly interpreted, even as its memory is being seared into the brains of the survivors.

It is important to draw a distinction between the *preservationist* communities of service that I am advocating, and mere *survivalist* communities. The latter exist primarily for the benefit of their members. Such communities will be regarded with suspicion and envy by others, and will be perpetually on the defensive. Preservationist communities, by contrast, will persist through acts of service that will make them indispensable to the regional population. Members of such communities will teach important skills — food growing and storage, tool and clothing making, house and boat building, renewable energy generation, and more; and provide healing, entertainment, general education, spiritual leadership and counseling, exchange depots for food and other commodities, seed banks, biodiversity refuges, and more. Survivalist communities will need to protect themselves from the people around them; preservationist communities will be protected by the people they serve.

Over time, generations issuing from the survivors will make what they will of the detritus of our civilization. Their recollection of it will inevitably become distorted, and they will adapt its remnant features to their needs. Important inventions will be forgotten, hard-won knowledge lost. Meanwhile, however, the human story will continue to unfold, and individuals of extraordinary intellect and talent will emerge to develop that story in ways unimaginable to us.

None of this may happen, however, if groups do not begin now to invest in acquiring the skills and infrastructure necessary. The sooner we build our lifeboats, the better off we will be.

CHAPTER SIX

Our Choice

*Again, in that day each little tribe will live by itself and
to itself and go its own way, and their differences will
soon be more than they were even in the first days of
[humankind], according to the accidents of survival
and of place . . . . In the distant years after these first
years, the tribes will grow more numerous and come
together, cross-fertilize in the body and in mind.*

—George R. Stewart, *Earth Abides* (1949)

*[P]erhaps our mission now is like that of the Native
Americans at the height of the genocide in the nineteenth century. At that point there was no question of
winning the battle. What remained to be done was to
keep hold of what it means to be human.*

—Stephanie Mills, *Epicurean Simplicity* (2002)

In the preceding chapters I have outlined a series of four options
for industrial societies, and individuals within those societies, as
the new century wears on — given the context of increasing population pressure and resource depletion, and the myriad of symptoms
issuing from those fundamental dilemmas. Of course, this cannot be

an exhaustive examination of the subject. What actually transpires in the decades ahead will probably be a surprising mix of the various possibilities outlined.

Many people will be unhappy with my delineation of these four options, and will say that I should have proposed others.

People on the right side of the political spectrum will likely regard my description of the Last One Standing option as a cynical view of the "War on Terror," and as a misrepresentation of America's noble aims in the Middle East.

People who identify with mainstream environmental, peace, and human rights organizations will say that I have made the Powerdown scenario sound far too difficult, thus dissuading readers from making efforts in that direction.

People from both ends of the political spectrum are likely to feel that my description of Waiting for the Magic Elixir is too pessimistically framed. I have subtitled it "Wishful Thinking, False Hopes, and Denial"; but what if some hopes are not false? More than a few readers will disagree with my unenthusiastic assessment of the hydrogen economy, or will choose to believe that a new invention will soon appear to solve humanity's resource problems.

Surely many readers will regard the very proposal of the option of Building Lifeboats as defeatist and gloomy. Suggesting that any of humanity's problems may be insoluble is bad form. When engaging in public discourse it is permissible to say, "If we don't do thus and so, terrible things will happen." This is the way in which discussions of global warming, nuclear proliferation, overpopulation, and other worrisome topics are typically framed. But even if the prescribed action is not being taken, and the world is in fact headed at top speed in the opposite direction, it is unacceptable to assume that the foreseen consequences will in fact appear, and to make plans accordingly.

Many readers will wonder why I didn't include a chapter on "Muddling Through": after all, humanity has heard dire warnings before, and yet we're still here. Others will be disappointed that there is no chapter on "Global Consciousness Change," describing how all our material difficulties will melt away if only we all adopt an enlightened spiritual worldview. I didn't include these chapters because "Muddling Through" is simply a variation of Waiting for the Magic Elixir, and the only Global Consciousness Change that would matter would be one that results in Powerdown; thus advocating Powerdown *is* advocating consciousness change. I suppose there could have been a chapter on the most obvious response to global resource depletion: eat, drink, and be merry. If there is little that we can do to reverse present trends, why not ignore them and have a good time? This is indeed an option, but it hardly deserves lengthy discussion. Those so inclined will be able to figure out the details of this strategy on their own.

There is, of course, quite a large group of people that believes the future will be far better than the present, and that no painful transition will be required. For them, my entire presentation is hopelessly wrongheaded. They might like to have seen a chapter on "Endless Economic Growth through Technological Progress," but that is for someone else's book. I simply do not agree that this is a likely outcome. It is easy to see why that message is always and everywhere welcome: we all love cheery news and an optimistic outlook. But the idea that we industrialized humans are immune to the natural laws that have restrained growth in other species, and humans in previous social regimes, is to me so self-servingly blind as to be morally reprehensible.

It is theoretically possible that our future will be shaped by unexpected revelations about space aliens. There are people who earnestly believe that this is true, but I do not have enough substantiated information on which to base any fixed opinion on the subject.

Then again, perhaps resource competition will never occur because humanity will first be wiped out by an overwhelming natural disaster, such as a collision with a comet or asteroid (yes, it could happen, and eventually will — though likely not for thousands or millions of years). This eventuality is of low probability in the short term, while the probabilities of the events I have been discussing — oil and natural gas depletion, tendencies toward increased geopolitical competition, widespread denial on the part of the majority of citizens, and the mounting of cooperative survival efforts by the few — have a probability so high as to approach certainty.

Is this fatalism? Far from it. Fatalism implies the absence of choice, while the entire point of my outlining these options is to highlight the choices available to us. True, our options are restricted, as they always are, by circumstance; wisdom ever lies in knowing the limits of choice and choosing well given those limits. Some limits — habits of mind and certain cultural barriers — we tend to accept too readily, and we need the courage to surmount them. Other limits — the ecological kind — we tend to ignore, all the while congratulating ourselves on our cleverness; these limits we must learn to respect.

OAEC: COMBINING POWERDOWN AND LIFEBOAT-BUILDING STRATEGIES

Located 65 miles north of San Francisco in western Sonoma County, the Occidental Arts and Ecology Center (OAEC) was founded in 1994 by a group of biologists, horticulturists, educators, activists, and artists seeking innovative and practical approaches to the pressing environmental and economic crises of our day. Part intentional community, part biodiversity preservation center, part activist training station, OAEC offers classes on starting and sustaining intentional communities, democratic decision-making, ecology, permaculture design, storm water management, sustainable forestry, school garden teacher training, and activist leadership training.

The organic gardens at OAEC grow thousands of rare and heirloom varieties of food plants; the garden staff, led by Master Gardener Doug Gosling, saves seeds each year and offers periodic plant sales to the general public as a way of helping preserve otherwise endangered varieties by increasing the number of growers.

In this final chapter we will examine these four options from three perspectives: that of the elites (governments, financial institutions, corporations, wealthy individuals); that of the organized opposition to the elites (the environmental, human rights, anti-globalization, and anti-war organizations and their allies); and finally, that of individuals who must sort out their alliances and interests on their own, and choose accordingly.

The Choice of the Elites

There is no need to belabor the point: the people of this world whose opinions count the most — the people with the power to command armies, economies, and governments — have already

Many of the structures on the property incorporate both traditional and visionary ecological building methods — cob, straw bale, thatch, natural plasters, and passive solar.

OAEC Director Dave Henson is a veteran activist in campaigns fighting corporate globalization and the genetic engineering of food plants, and supporting related environmental and human-rights issues. He is a contributor to the book *Fatal Harvest: The Tragedy of Industrial Agriculture* (Island Press, 2002), and is a member of the think tank, Program on Corporations, Law, and Democracy (POCLAD).

Henson and others offer periodic trainings to "organize people and communities around strategic campaigns that go to the root causes of the destruction of watersheds, biological diversity, local economic sustainability, and human communities."

OAEC members manage to serve the surrounding community, preserve life-sustaining knowledge and skills, and foment social change simultaneously — while also having a rollicking good time: the yearly schedule also includes parties, plays, and concerts.

For further information: <www.oaec.org>.

made up their minds. The cards are dealt and the bets are on the table. For them, the coming decades will constitute a fatal game of Last One Standing, a brutal contest for the world's remaining resources.

To the interested observer, this may seem patently insane. Even the nation that "wins" the game will be utterly devastated. In the end, oil, natural gas, and even coal will run out, and not even the wealthy will be able to maintain their current way of life. And in the meantime, hundreds of millions — perhaps billions — will have violently perished. *Why would anyone choose this path?*

It is possible to understand the reason for the current course of events only by looking at *who* is choosing it, and at the incentives and constraints to which they are subject.

The elites — corporate owners and managers, government officials, and military commanders — are people who have been selected for certain qualities: loyalty to the system, competitiveness, and hunger for power. Often they are literally bred for their roles. Like George W. Bush, they are people born to wealth and power, and raised to assume that privilege is their birthright. These are people who identify with the system and the status quo; they are constitutionally incapable of questioning its fundamental assumptions.

Moreover, the elites are guided day-to-day by a set of incentives that are built into the system itself. Managers who pursue immediate gain get ahead, while those who make short-term sacrifices in order to preserve long-term stability are often at a disadvantage. Likewise, managers are rewarded who keep up appearances, who generate good news, and who exude confidence. Confessing errors accrues no benefit; instead, managers are encouraged to deny shortcomings and to blame competitors or subordinates.

Such conduct is hardly unique to the elites; everyone behaves in this fashion from time to time. But the system, in grooming its most prominent caretakers, selects for these behaviors; it carefully fosters some personality types and excludes others: assertive individuals who think concretely come to the fore, while creative dreamers fall by the wayside.

Leaders are often good liars: they are people who have learned how to tell others what they want to hear. We voters tend to elect and follow such people. Even if we know at some level that we are being lied to, we are flattered and pleasantly illusioned (we hate being dis-illusioned). The best liars are able to convince themselves of the truth of what they are saying, so that, in their own minds, they are not lying at all; as a result they can be eminently convincing. J. P. Morgan (who knew something about power and influence) once said that "A man generally has two reasons for doing a thing: one that sounds good, and a real one." Some of us are very good at deluding ourselves that the reason that sounds good *is* the real one.[1]

Such elemental human foibles shape not just the details but also the grand arc of history. President Clinton exhibited a highly developed ability to lie convincingly (perhaps even to himself) in his creative redefinition of extramarital sex; of far more consequence, during the buildup to the recent American-British invasion of Iraq, the neoconservative policymakers of the Bush administration were widely observed to select and publicize intelligence reports that supported their worldview, and to disregard others that challenged it. They were evidently more interested in furthering their preconceived agenda than in gaining an accurate picture of the world and of the likely effects of their actions. This attitude came back to bite them when forecasts of an easy invasion and a friendly reception by the Iraqi people gave way to the reality of protracted guerilla war. Early warnings of the latter outcome from CIA and State Department analysts had been shunted aside by neoconservative policymakers who refused to think that the invasion could turn sour, and therefore failed to plan for the possibility.

Moreover, the war had been "sold" to the public as necessary in order to root out illegal Iraqi weapons of mass destruction, which UN weapons inspectors were purportedly too incompetent to locate. When, following the invasion, a massive search by US military and intelligence officers likewise failed to uncover banned weapons, the rationale for the invasion shifted retroactively: it had never really been about WMDs; the purpose had always been to rid the Iraqi people of their hated dictator. The mendacity was breath-taking. As Dennis Cass put it in his article "Whoppers of Mass Destruction" (*Mother Jones,* June 23), "When Defense Secretary Donald Rumsfeld says, 'I don't believe anyone that I know in the administration ever said that Iraq had nuclear weapons,' it astounds the senses on a cellular level." Yet in hearing members of the administration deliver their ever-shifting explanations during the autumn of 2003, I was struck by the perception that these people often seemed to *believe* what they were saying. It was as though they had developed uniquely flexible mental muscles that permitted them to earnestly hold as true whatever view of reality seemed convenient or profitable in the moment — regardless of its utter incompatibility with the view that had been held the day before.

While the neoconservatives may have an extreme (perhaps fatal) case of this curious self-deception syndrome, it is a common malady of those in power — hence the fairy tale of the emperor's new clothes, and the old tradition of killing the messenger who brings bad news.

There are always plenty of messengers available to tell the elites what they would like to believe. The late economist Julian Simon made a career of it, and his spirit is alive and well among legions of futurists who proclaim that a continually burgeoning human population is not a problem but an advantage, and that our particular civilization is uniquely immune to resource limits. Their message always has an audience, and often a well-paying audience — after all, a general atmosphere of optimism is good for both votes and share prices.

Managers know that if they try to alter the basic parameters by which the system operates, the system will simply eject them. Leaders can make adjustments, but only minor ones. This is less the case when systems are new and still in the process of being designed; but once a social establishment has been in place for many decades it becomes highly resistant to change — or, more accurately, *change of certain kinds.* Dramatic change that merely exacerbates ongoing trends (such as a steeply increasing accumulation of power and wealth by a tiny minority), can often be tolerated, while moderate change that undercuts fundamental trends (such as an effort to seriously limit resource usage), is typically vigorously discouraged.

And so we find ourselves in a social system that knows only how to grow, and that would rather violently explode than deliberately contract; and with leaders who have been selected precisely for their willingness and ability to carry out the system's operating instructions, however ultimately self-destructive they may be. The system needs petroleum, but indigenous reserves are quickly depleting. There is more oil elsewhere. For the leaders, there is only one possible solution: get that oil, whatever the cost. Never mind that the cost may include invasions, military occupations, and eventually, perhaps, total war.

There are disagreements among the elites. Billionaire investor George Soros has said that it is currently his life's goal to unseat the neoconservatives in Washington. He evidently believes that the current administration is pursuing the growth imperative far too recklessly; as a result, the system may come apart at the seams sooner rather than later.

Even within the Bush administration there have allegedly been rifts. With Afghanistan and Iraq in turmoil, and with the 2004 elections looming, power appears to be shifting from the neocon hawks in the Defense Department to "realists" in the State Department, who advocate wrapping up the Iraq fiasco, withdrawing as quickly as possible, and moving on to other business. However, abandoning Iraq now will merely necessitate further military intervention in the region later, so it is likely that a compromise will be worked out — or that a stalemate will ensue . . . or that the area of disagreement is actually smaller than some have suggested.

In addition, elites in many countries smaller than the US are showing signs of unease with the Last One Standing strategy and have announced that they might wish to undertake some form of Powerdown. For example, the government of Iceland has declared that it intends to wean itself from petroleum entirely within the next few decades. No doubt the Icelanders would like to see international treaties enacted that would set the rest of the world on the same path. But they have indigenous geothermal energy resources that could enable a relatively gentle energy transition in their country; the US is not in so favorable a position. Iceland has a tiny military; America's is formidable.

George Soros may be successful in rendering jobless the current occupant of the White House; and even if Bush stays for another term, the influence of the neoconservative hawks may be on the wane. But the new leader or advisers will undoubtedly pursue policies similar to the current ones in their ultimate goals, if gentler in their execution, simply because US policymakers are not even contemplating a serious Powerdown strategy and, in the end, the only alternative to Powerdown is more competition, which will eventually lead to more war and more repression. Meanwhile the quiet voices of countries, like Iceland, that may wish to lead the world toward a cooperative Powerdown, will almost certainly be drowned out by the war cries of incomparably more menacing countries that have decided to maximize their energy flow-through rates and ruthlessly compete for the resources needed to continue increasing consumption rates for as long as possible. While the US and China remain on a collision course, what everyone else does is beside the point. Only after the inevitable cataclysm might the advantage go to the meek.

For now, from the vantage point of the controlling elites, whether by deliberation or by default, cutthroat competition is the order of the day, and whoever flinches first merely seals his fate.

The Choice of the Movement

The world's environmental, anti-war, anti-globalization, and human rights organizations (which came to be called "the Other Superpower" during the vast anti-war demonstrations of the spring of 2003 — but which, for the sake of brevity, I will refer to simply as "the Movement"), have a radically different view of the situation from that of the ruling elites. The Movement's primary interest is in dispersing power and wealth, rather than further concentrating them; in preventing war and countering political repression; and in protecting the Earth's fragile ecosystems.

Unfortunately, the tide of history is currently moving the other way — toward more consolidation of power and wealth, toward the development and dispersal of ever more horrific weapons, and toward increased rates of resource extraction and environmental destruction. The Movement's response is not to give up, but to push harder, while maintaining the moral high ground. The task of changing the direction of events may appear hopeless; nevertheless, in the view of Movement leaders, opposing war and oppression is the right thing to do, regardless of the odds. Mahatma Gandhi and Martin Luther King confronted entrenched patterns of social inequity, and at first their efforts to change these patterns seemed hopeless to many. But by perseverance, and by moral example and persuasion, they prevailed. The leaders of the Movement take the same attitude today: however daunting their undertaking may appear, the alternative — allowing the world to slide further into war, tyranny, and environmental ruin — is simply unacceptable.

The Movement has a blind spot, however: while it addresses a wide range of issues related to militarism, inequality, environmental depredation, and injustice, it cannot easily speak to resource and population issues. That is because Movement leaders — like the leaders of established governmental, economic, and military institutions — are vulnerable to political incentives and constraints that prevent them from coming to grips with the most fundamental facts about our species-wide ecological dilemma.

For Movement leaders, the primary incentive must be to attract the interest and loyalty of multitudes. Since the Movement lacks formal political power, only the support of the masses can give it potency. There is a further incentive: it is highly desirable for all of the various issue organizations of the Movement (organizations to clean up toxic waste, to save endangered species, to ban land mines, to promote minority rights, to oppose military aggression, and on and on), to work together, and to present a united front. United, they are powerful; divided, they are like so many gnats pestering the elite-driven Leviathan.

However, some of the organizations making up the Movement — principally the human rights and environmental organizations — actually have diverging interests. Human rights workers deal with immediate, concrete instances of repression and atrocity. They take a principled stand, but with a very few exceptions are disinclined to take a long view with regard to population and resource issues. Environmentalists often have a better understanding of population and resources: they see how closely every impending ecological catastrophe is related to the burgeoning human population. A few environmentalists go further in their thinking and draw connections between population pressure and resource depletion on one hand, and war and economic exploitation on the other.

This difference in emphasis may seem fairly trivial when stated this way, but, as we are about to see, it is crucial. The nub of the problem is this: The population issue is problematic from a human-rights perspective, because no one has yet been able to envision a way of significantly reducing the total human population of the planet over the course of the next few decades without resorting to some method that would compromise what many regard as the most sacred of human rights — the right to reproduce. So, for the sake of solidarity and mutual support, the two sets of organizations tend to downplay their differences. But this requires that environmental organizations refrain from speaking frankly about one of the central problems of our era.

By any reasonable assessment, the Earth has already exceeded its carrying capacity for humans: every basic means of life-support (including the world's oceans, topsoils, and fresh water systems) appears to be in the beginning stages of collapse. The depletion of fossil fuels will put much more pressure on the global ecosystem's ability to sustain a large human population, since currently much of that population is supported by industrial agriculture and the long-distance transportation of food and other resources from regions where they are abundant to places where they are scarce; and, as we have seen, transportation and industrial agriculture are highly vulnerable to reduced fuel inputs. As mentioned in the Introduction, just since 1998 (when the global population reached 6 billion) we have added yet another 400 million to the total — nearly the population of North America. Where is the support system for these people? It is ludicrous to think of the world finding a North America's worth of resources, and building a North America's worth of support infra-structure every six years in order to support the human lives added through current rates of population growth. Thus, more population growth just means more poverty, more misery.

Ultimately, ignoring the population issue will be a catastrophe for human rights, since population pressure is reliably one of the pri-mary drivers of environmental destruction. With continued popula-tion growth, ever more resource competition will become inevitable, even in the face of heroic efforts to fairly redistribute whatever resources are still available. The Movement seeks peace, freedom, equality, and justice. But with too many people trying to inhabit a finite planet, the ecological requirements for these desir-able conditions will vanish. Ecologists familiar with human history (and historians familiar with the principles of ecology) know that peace, cooperation, equity, and justice are most easily realized in a condition in which population is low relative to the available resources (though there have been exceptions).[2] The Industrial Revolution simply added a new twist to this rule: the drawdown of fossil fuels temporarily enabled us to extract and transport other resources at a faster rate, so as to create "phantom" carrying capac-ity. As the remainder of Earth's finite gift of fossil fuels is burned, that new, temporary carrying capacity will disappear; and as biolog-ical support systems are further damaged by the demands of over-populated industrial societies, we may see Earth's baseline carrying capacity for humans plummet.

But the best the Movement can do is to plead for a "stabiliza-tion" of human population at around 7.4 billion — the low range of UN estimates for 2050 — through the means of educating women and distributing birth control information and devices. These methods should certainly be pursued, but will they be enough to prevent a human and environmental catastrophe? If the

Earth is barely — and only temporarily — able to support the current human population, even with the gift of cheap fossil fuels, then a mere "stabilization" of human numbers is no solution.

Environmentalists typically agree to soft-pedal the population issue not only because it conflicts with the views of human-rights activists, but also because population reduction is hard to sell to the general public. People just don't want to hear about it. The simple distribution of birth-control devices and information is already politically problematic because of pressures from the Catholic Church and US political reactionaries. Thus even population "stabilization" is a contentious issue and tends to be downplayed. To speak of an actual *reduction* of human population — exactly what is needed if the world is to avoid unprecedented human dieoff through famine, pestilence, and war — is unthinkable and unspeakable, at least in polite company. Not just Catholics and conservatives, but liberals as well become positively apoplectic if the subject is broached.

And so the discussion necessary to understanding our ecological dilemma, and dealing effectively with it, never occurs.[3]

The Movement also, though to a lesser degree, soft-pedals per-capita resource consumption issues. The current level of economic inequity in the world, and within many countries, is astonishing. A mere 500 people — the world's richest — control as much wealth as the poorer half of humanity. The Movement rightly highlights this inequality and demands some sort of wealth redistribution. Sometimes Movement leaders go so far as to say that the wasteful lifestyles of people in the industrialized world — and here they refer principally to the US and Canada — must change, because the world doesn't have enough resources to enable everyone to live like a typical North American. This is a point that needs stressing. Human impact on the environment is not measured by population levels alone, but by population multiplied by per-capita resource consumption. If we are to navigate the next few decades peaceably, we must both reduce population *and* reduce per-capita resource usage in both the wealthier countries and the wealthier segments of poor countries.

But this latter message doesn't always go down well with North Americans who have grown accustomed to their consumptive habits. And it is North Americans and Europeans who provide most of the funding for the Movement's various organizations. And so the politically acceptable prescription from the Movement's more mainstream organizations tends to be, *raise living standards in poor countries.* This benign-sounding strategy goes by the name "development," and it is virtually sacrosanct among non-governmental organizations. In practical effect, development has meant turning poor nations into shabby imitations of rich ones, building cities on the industrial model while undermining traditional subsistence agriculture. It has been a tragedy for indigenous, sustainable cultures worldwide, and the resulting teeming urban centers will likely be sites of immense human tragedy in the decades ahead. What is needed is not the further "development" of the poor countries, but the systematic and intelligent de-industrialization of both rich and poor ones.

If we were living in a world that weren't on the brink of resource depletion and environmental collapse, then we might envision a win-win scenario in which rich nations could keep their two-car lifestyle, while countries like China and India could gradually come up to speed, with formerly poor families gradually acquiring washing machines, cars, and microwave ovens until they, too, lived a version of the American dream. But that is a fantasy world. The reality is that *no* country will be able to maintain a quasi-American lifestyle for its citizens past the first or second decade of this century. Someone must tell the Chinese to abandon their dreams of owning BMWs, and someone must tell Americans to ditch their SUVs and start growing backyard gardens.

But woe to the messenger. People in the poorer countries understandably resent being told that they will never enjoy the comforts that Americans and Europeans take for granted. And of course Americans prefer to think that, as their president has told them, their current way of life is "non-negotiable." Whenever the population/resource discussion begins, it tends quickly to devolve into a bout of finger-pointing: North Americans highlight the overpopulation of poor countries of Africa and Asia, but tend to overlook their own unsustainable levels of resource consumption. Meanwhile, Movement leaders from the poorer countries tend to focus on the global inequity of per-capita resource consumption, and to ignore the population issue. Each side is correct in its criticism of the other: North Americans' and Europeans' rates of consumption contribute to making their own countries dramatically overpopulated (since overpopulation, like human environmental impact, is a function of sheer human numbers multiplied by per-capita rates of resource consumption); meanwhile, the overpopulation of a country like India is not due simply to the fact that rich Westerners are soaking up most of the world's resources: India's ecosystems are collapsing and famine appears increasingly likely as food production in that country begins to decline.

The world must do both — reduce human population *and* reduce per-capita resource consumption in the industrialized regions — if society is to power down rather than collapse in chaos. The Earth cannot afford rich people, nor can it continuously support six billion humans and counting at *any* standard of living.

But this news pleases no one. If the Movement were to truly embrace it, the elites would pounce, and it would be the easiest PR takedown in history. A few well-paid public relations firms would place some ads and op-ed pieces, and an "authoritative" study or two would be issued saying, in effect, "Nonsense! There is plenty for everyone; technology and the market will fix everything." Broadcast commentators would pile on, polls would be taken, and the foolish notion that humans actually face ecological constraints, just as all other organisms do, would be thoroughly discredited and banished from serious conversation. Imagine how the talk show hosts would rant: "Reduce our standard of living? Now 'they' are trying to take away your car!" — a car that will cease to run anyway when oil becomes prohibitively expensive. "Reduce population? Why that sounds like genocide!" — which, ironically, is exactly what the elites themselves are preparing for through their investments in nuclear bombs and genetic bio-weapons.

And so the critical message is muted and truncated. The Movement tailors its utterances for maximum public-relations effectiveness, just as the elites do. Politics trumps truth.

Even though the Movement calls for Powerdown, what is being suggested is not a strategy that could actually succeed; rather, it is Powerdown Lite, a soft and toothless version that, if enacted, would only slightly postpone the human dieoff. Instead of calling for a massive reduction in energy usage by industrial societies, Movement leaders sing the praises of the illusory hydrogen economy. They promote the reasonable idea that that there will be enough for everyone, as long as goods are fairly distributed — but omit the other necessary conditional phrase: *if human numbers are kept within the long-term carrying capacity of the environment and human demands are kept modest.*

I am pounding on this point because it is not an incidental one. Population pressure and resource depletion are not side issues; they are *the* issues. The Movement largely ignores the core dilemma facing humanity because it has no politically agreeable solution for it. The elites have no solution either, but they do have a fallback strategy: competition, repression, and war. It is a terrible strategy, and someone needs to propose a workable alternative. Instead, what we get is a greenish version of Waiting for the Magic Elixir.

Perhaps I am being unfair. The Movement is at least pushing more or less in the right direction, and what it proposes is certainly better than nothing. But I find it disappointing to watch many leaders of the Movement subject themselves to a pattern of self-deception similar to that prevailing among the elites. In this case, the incentives and constraints are different, but in one respect the result is the same: almost no one speaks frankly about the crisis ahead of us.

The Choice of Us Folks

The great majority of people in the world today are sympathetic to the views either of the elites or of the Movement, because these are the views presented via the mass media. Of course, the elites have the upper hand in this regard, because they control much of the media content.

Individuals — especially in the US — who feel a strong sense of loyalty to the governing elites, or who harbor profound feelings of "patriotism" (which, these days, seems to mean the same thing), or whose primary incentive is to preserve current social conditions, may understandably gravitate toward leaders who promise to protect and preserve the status quo by maintaining access to resources and defeating foreigners who threaten that access. This group is largely made up of people from the wealthier social strata, those who are old enough to have families and to have built up a reasonable pile of possessions, and people of all ages and wealth strata whose world-view is shaped primarily by television. These folks will reflexively respond to the strategy of Last One Standing.

Following the elites' lead, they will find themselves in a world that doesn't respond the way it is supposed to. Wars of "liberation"

EDUCATION FOR SOCIAL CHANGE AND CULTURAL RENEWAL

New College of California is an accredited school founded in 1971, whose mission is to "integrate education with the creation of a just, sacred, and sustainable world." Among the offerings at the main campus in San Francisco is a program in Humanities with an emphasis in Activism and Social Change, "designed to address the educational needs and social concerns of both aspiring and engaged activists."

The North Bay campus of New College, where I teach, located in Santa Rosa, focuses especially on ecological issues in its Culture, Ecology, and Sustainable Community program, whose purpose is to help students

- Overcome alienation and heal both people and the Earth.
- Resist further destruction of people and planet.

may continue to devolve into long, bloody military occupations and endless "terrorism." The economy will unwind even though those in charge claim to be doing all the right things. The only way to make sense of the events will be to assume that malevolent groups and individuals are foiling the well-laid, beneficent plans of the elites. Thus, the preservation of civilization as we know it will require the rooting out of these evil ones; and since their wickedness knows no bounds, our fearless leaders will be justified in using any and all tactics to oppose them. We citizens will have to sacrifice much of our humanity, and many of our ideals, in order to wage this great holy battle. Folks who follow the elites will have to give up a great deal — but they will get to keep their sense of entitlement and righteousness.

Those who have reason to question the elites' strategies — including some people from poorer social strata, leftist intellectuals, and those most directly affected by environmental collapse — will

---

- Build sustainable, alternative ways of living.
- Create a shift in the culture's consciousness to a more holistic, ecological paradigm.
- Build community in an increasingly isolating and individualizing culture.

The North Bay Campus offers a Green MBA program, in which students learn how to create and manage sustainable local enterprises, as well as concentrations in eco-dwelling, ecological agriculture, nutrition, and consciousness, healing and ecology.

Undergraduate and graduate students at New College North Bay gather on weekends to learn theory and skills, and go on to design their own year-long, depth-learning project.

For more information:
<www.newcollege.edu/northbay/index.html>.

respond to a set of incentives that draw them in the general direction of the Powerdown strategy, though again, they are likely to contemplate only a watered-down version of it.

The folks who choose the Powerdown path are in for disappointment on two sides: the elites will likely refuse to change course, while the world continues to fragment; and they will know that they have answers to the world's problems, but will see few of their solutions implemented. They will commiserate among themselves at how inept and self-serving the elites are, and will pay rapt attention to the deepening poverty and environmental ruin around them. The more radical of these folks will be demonized and persecuted by the elites; they will also be subject to burnout, as they make heroic efforts to stop the violence and aid the victims. But they will get to keep their idealism, and any victory they achieve along the way will be worth savoring.

The majority of both groups will feel attracted to the path of Waiting for the Magic Elixir. Everyone wants solutions — the easier the better. Even an unworkable solution is better than none at all. However, those who anticipate salvation from technology or the market will find themselves waiting . . . and waiting. The solution will seem obvious — why hasn't it been adopted? As the years go by they will wonder whatever happened to the hydrogen economy, or the Canadian tar sands, or methane hydrates, or thermal depolymerization. Seeing the world situation worsen, they will look for scapegoats either among the elites ("those wretched oil companies are polluting the air and commandeering our foreign policy — while suppressing promising new technologies that could save the world!"), or the Movement ("those damned environmentalists are keeping us from developing nuclear power and are weakening our national resolve!"). In order to continue believing in easy solutions, these folks will have to sacrifice their capacity for critical thinking. But they will get to keep their optimism.

A small minority — people who are at the margins of the system and who are thus able to observe it as if from outside, who are not tied into any of the major influence groups, and who have learned to seek out alternative sources of information and think critically — will gradually come to the conclusion that the entire system of industrial civilization is inherently unsustainable. Of that group, most will simply watch helplessly and cynically as the world disintegrates. Only a small subset of this already marginal group will have the wherewithal to actually build effective cultural lifeboats.

Lifeboat builders will face their own challenges. The elites will see them as outsiders and therefore as potential "terrorists," while the Movement will view them as self-absorbed survivalists (which, in some instances, will likely be true). The lifeboat builders will be trying to construct small, local, sustainable social systems in the context of a world that is tearing such systems apart in its futile attempts to push the strategy of globalization to its bitter conclusion. They will have only a small constituency of supporters and will have to overcome tendencies toward cynicism. But they will get to keep their realism, their creativity, and their autonomy.

The situation is not cut-and-dried, however. Many people will be drawn in more than one direction — seeing evidence that our current brand of industrialism is unsustainable, but recoiling at the thought that it cannot be salvaged in some form. These folks will likely be drawn toward some combination of lifeboat-building and Powerdown — working for change within the system while also making other plans.

I personally am drawn to this combined strategy for the following reasons. I believe that the building of cultural lifeboats is essential if there is even a moderate likelihood of the collapse of industrial civilization. And, as should be clear by now, it seems to me that the likelihood of this is more than moderate. However, if any shred of the Powerdown strategy succeeds, it will help make the collapse slower and gentler, thus reducing suffering and environmental damage, and buying time for more lifeboat building. I also believe that a good case can be made for taking the moral high ground and fighting the good fight for peace, social justice, and environmental protection, even if many of the battles along the way are sure to be lost.

I am reminded of events in Cuba during the Special Period: a small group of agronomists had been advocating ecological agriculture for years previously, with no success; but when oil imports fell and the Cuban economy teetered, the nation's political leaders called on these marginalized ecological agronomists to redesign the country's food system. Something similar could happen globally in the years ahead. Perhaps when economies are shattered by the effects of oil and natural gas depletion, the prophets of Powerdown — who are today relegated to the fringes — will be called upon to implement some of their plans for conservation and redistribution. Then all of their previously thankless analysis and planning will finally pay off.

I am reminded also of friends in several intentional communities and ecovillages around the world who have likewise decided to pursue Powerdown and lifeboat-building strategies simultaneously. While they engage in activism on many fronts — participating vigorously in the anti-globalization, peace, and environmental movements — they also have established rural bases where they save heirloom seeds, build their own homes from natural and locally-available materials, and hone other life-support skills that they and future generations will need. I admire these people unreservedly: if there is a sane path from where we are to a truly sustainable future, these folks have surely found it.

Looking Ahead

We face the most important and difficult choices in human history. It would be reassuring to think that we are making them with our eyes open, with the options clearly laid out, and with the consequences of various paths well understood.

For the vast majority of the world's people, however, this is far from being the case. I hope that this book can help to clarify our situation and the alternative actions available. Of course, in the end, this is just one person's attempt to survey a vast, complex, and shifting terrain, and I have inevitably oversimplified it. The view I have offered is unavoidably partial, even though my goal has been to set aside personal prejudices as much as I can.

Assuming that one has opted to avoid denial and wishful think-ing, there is a tendency to view our collective prospects with fatalism, pessimism, or despair. But these attitudes are of help to no one. A keener awareness of our dilemma is of little use unless we are able to employ that awareness constructively. I hope that the analysis in this book will enable activists to direct their efforts more strategically; and community leaders to make more realistic and immediate plans for disaster preparedness, and to begin rebuilding an infrastructure for local food and energy self-sufficiency. I wish that all who read this book will be motivated to make personal life choices that will lead them to survive and be of service to others during the transition peri-od we are entering.

I also hope this book can help people better understand the con-text of their lives, so that they can respond intelligently and com-passionately to the emerging challenges, rather than falling prey to finger-pointing and scapegoating. As we enter what are likely to be the most difficult of times, we must make deliberate efforts to pre-serve our highest human values and ideals. When the ratio of human population to available resources becomes less favorable, human life may begin to appear cheap and superfluous, and fear and hate may seem justified. Sadly, we are already beginning to see an increase in these attitudes. In America especially, hate has been palpably on the rise for the past dozen years or so. It is not unusual to hear "shock jocks" on talk radio advocate "head shots" when speaking of certain politicians, or the equivalent of ethnic cleansing or religious war when discussing people of Middle Eastern descent. The shrill voices of these disturbingly popular commentators appeal to the ugliest aspects of the human character, and media moguls have unfortu-nately discovered that hate sells.

We learned from the Nazi experiment of the 1930s that, in a modern industrial society, hate — if supported by governmental authority and the use of modern communications media — can become a kind of mental virus that can afflict nearly an entire popu-lation. We learned that hate can kill, and that, when it infects an entire society, it can kill in huge numbers.

Intense stress sometimes brings out the worst in people — and sometimes the best. There is no path ahead that does not entail extraordinary cultural stress, and we must choose how to deal with it. May we choose not only with eyes that are open, but with hearts that are strong and open.

NOTES

Introduction

1. "The deep oceans are warming, the tundra is thawing, the glaciers are melting, infectious diseases are migrating, and the timing of the seasons has changed. All that has resulted from only one degree [Fahrenheit, 0.6 degrees Celsius] of warming. It is expected that the earth will warm another three to 10 degrees later in this century, according to the UN-sponsored Intergovernmental Panel on Climate Change (IPCC)." Ross Gelbspan, "Toward a Global Energy Transition," PFIF Petropolitics Special Report. <www.fpif.org/papers/03petropol/alternatives.html>. See also various articles on the Woods Hole Oceanographic Institute "Abrupt Climate Change" web site. <www.whoi.edu/institutes/occi/currenttopics/ ct_abruptclimate.htm>.

2. At the end of 1993, "The total national debt of the United States on a fully realized basis, inclusive of federal, state, county and local debt stood at a record $20.613 trillion (83.73% of said debt having been created from 1981–92 and from 2001 to present.) The total public and private indebtedness of the United States ended the year 2003 at $39.384 trillion. The total public and private assets of the United States ended the year 2003 at $26.134 trillion. Thus, the United States by the

end of 2003 has a negative net worth of approximately $13 trillion. The total debt service of the United States ended the year 2003 at 309.4% of GDP (Gross Domestic Product). These are numbers never before seen. This is a higher debt to gross domestic product ratio than [that of] any other country on earth, which still services its debt. For instance this is a higher fraction of debt service to GDP than [that of] the government of Nigeria. The United States federal government, as of the end of 2003, was servicing 41.3% of total debt — the only first-world nation on the planet that services less than 100% of its debt." "Scoreboard 2003," by Al Martin, <www.almartinraw.com> accessed January 12, 2004.

3. <http://news.independent.co.uk/uk/environment/story.jsp?story=454828>.

4. Joseph Tainter, *The collapse of Complex Societies*. Cambridge University Press, 1988.

Chapter 1: The End of Cheap Energy

1. Based on personal communication with Gregson Vaux, SAIC Power/Energy Engineer at the National Energy Technology Laboratory, and author of a forthcoming study on coal.

2. Jon Thompson, "A Revolutionary Transformation," *The Lamp*, Vol. 85, No.1.

3. Richard Duncan, "Three World Oil Forecasts Predict Peak Oil Production," *Oil & Gas Journal*, May 26, 2003, pp. 18-21.

4. Russell Brown, "Critical Paths to the Post-Petroleum Age," cited in *ASPO News* No. 35, November 2003. <www.asponews.org/docs/Newsletter35.doc>.

5. Zittel and Schindler, "Future World Oil Supply," <www.peakoil.net/Publications/International-Summer-School_Salzburg_2002.pdf>.

6. Peter Calamai, "Energy crisis looms, experts warn: Worldwide oil, gas production expected to peak in 2020; Only solution to impending shortage will be higher prices." *Toronto Star*, November 26, 2003.

7. <http://www.wtrg.com/oecd/OECD0304.html>.

8.   See "Oil Reserves Sink; Heating Costs Rise," Gannett News
     Service, January 7, 2004, <http://www.qctimes.com/inter-
     nal.php?story_id=1022658&t=Business&c=31,1022658>.

9.   "Strategic Energy Policy Challenges for the 21st Century,"
     Report of an Independent Task Force sponsored by the James
     A. Baker Institute for Policy of Rice University and the
     Council on Foreign Relations, p. 19.
     <www.bakerinstitute.org/Pubs/studies/bipp_study_15/bipp-
     study15.html>.

10. Op. cit., p. 4.

11. See "Revising the forecasts for Saudi oil," *The Daily Star,*
     Beirut, Dec. 15, 2003. <http://www.dailystar.com.lb/opin-
     ion/17_11_03_c.asp>.

12. The *Independent,* UK, "Oil and gas running out much faster
     than expected, says study" by Charles Arthur, October 2,
     2003.

13. *Nature,* November 20, 2003, Vol. 426, pp. 318-322.

14. From a News Release of the Oil Depletion Analysis Centre
     (London), February 9, 2004. <www.odac-info.org/>.

15. Wood MacKenzie, "New Thinking Needed for Exploration,"
     January 4, 2004. <www.woodmac.com/enhorizons.htm#new-
     thinking>.

16. Andrew McKillop, *The Final Energy Crisis,* unpublished as of
     this writing. <http://solutions.synearth.net/2003/12/02>.

17. Bloomberg, January 9, 2004.
     <http://209.157.64.200/focus/f-news/1054647/posts>.

18. "Russian oil and gas sector growth may stop in 2007," RBC
     News, January 13, 2004. "According to LUKoil Vice
     President Leonid Fedun, by 2007 the Russian oil and gas sec-
     tor will stop rising. This announcement came as a comment
     on LUKoil's intention to refrain from a large-scale step-up in
     oil production. LUKoil expects its oil output to grow by 4
     percent to 85m tons this year. Last year LUKoil's oil output
     increased by 2.1 percent to 81.5m tons."
     <www.rbcnews.com/free/20040113182855.shtml>.

19. For a discussion of peak in net energy see *The Party's Over*, pp. 202–203.

20. <www.eia.gov>.

21. <www.cia.gov>.

22. This is, of course, a somewhat simplistic generalization, as some people tend to think ahead more than others. Foresightedness is no doubt encouraged or discouraged by cultural and environmental factors as well as by genetics. Nevertheless, the innate "fight or flight" response is clearly geared toward immediate threats, and it is seldom activated by developing long-term problems that require intellectual analysis — such as global climate change or impending (though not immediate) resource shortages. For a discussion of this issue, see Reg Morrison, *The Spirit in the Gene: Humanity's Proud Illusion and the Laws of Nature*. Cornell University Press, 1999.

23. <www.financialsense.com/editorials/powers/2004/0104.html>.

24. USGS Fact Sheet 123-00, "Coal-bed Methane: Potential and Concerns". <http://pubs.usgs.gov/fs/fs123-00/fs123-00.pdf>.

25. "U.S. calls for creation of global natural gas industry" December 19, 2003. <www.arabicnews.com/ansub/Daily/Day/031219/2003121934.html>.

26. Julian Darley, *High Noon for Natural Gas*. Chelsea Green, in press.

Chapter 2: Last One Standing

1. Raymond C. Kelly, *Warless Societies and the Origins of War*. University of Michigan Press, 2000.

2. Summary by Dennis Avery, "Why the World Used to Have More Wars," Center for Global Food Issues. <www.cgfi.org/materials/articles/2003/may_07_03.htm>.

3. For example, see John Chuckman, "It's Not About Oil," <www.rense.com/general33/notabout.htm>.

4. Adam Smith, *Wealth of Nations*, Modern Library ed. Random House, 1965, p. 642.

5. Project for a New American Century, "Rebuilding America's Defenses: Strategies, Forces And Resources For A New Century." <www.newamericancentury.org/ RebuildingAmericasDefenses.pdf>.

6. "Strategic Energy Policy Challenges for the 21st Century," Report of an Independent Task Force sponsored by the James A. Baker Institute for Policy of Rice University and the Council on Foreign Relations. <www.bakerinstitute.org/ Pubs/studies/bipp_study_15/bippstudy15.html>.

7. Judicial Watch web site. <www.judicialwatch.org/071703.b_PR.shtml>.

8. Associated Press, "U.S. Considered Oil Invasion in 1973, Britain Says," January 1, 2004.

9. See, for example, Nafeez Mosaddeq Ahmed, *Behind the War on Terror: Western Secret Strategy and the Struggle for Iraq.* New Society, 2003.

10. See Greg Palast, *The Best Democracy Money Can Buy: An Investigative Reporteer Exposes the Truth about Globalization, Corporate Cons, and High Finance Fraudsters.* Pluto Press, 2002.

11. George Freimoth, "The Return of Cold War 'Terrorists,'" Marin Interfaith Task Force on Central America newsletter, Spring 2002. <www.thirdworldtraveler.com/ Terrorism/ Cold_War_Terrorists.html>.

12. See also Eric Hofschmid, *Painful Questions: An Analysis of the September 11th Attack.* Endpoint Software, 2002. <www.fromthewilderness.com>; <www.cooperativeresearch.org>; <www.globalresearch.ca>; <www.whatreallyhappened.com>.

13. The Carnegie Endowment for International Peace, "Report says Iraq didn't have WMD," released January 8, 2004. <www.cnn.com/2004/US/01/08/sprj.nirq.wmd.report/ index.html>.

14. In January 2001, the European Parliament approved a resolution imposing a ban on the use of DU munitions while investigations were carried out into the links between DU and cancer.

In August 2002, the UN published a report citing a series of international laws and conventions breached by the use of DU weapons, including: the Universal Declaration of Human Rights; the UN Charter; the UN Genocide Convention; the Convention Against Torture; the four Geneva Conventions of 1949; the Conventional Weapons Convention of 1980; and the Hague Conventions of 1899 and 1907 which all forbid the deployment of "poison or poisoned weapons" and "arms, projectiles or materials calculated to cause unnecessary suffering."

15. See: <www.mindfully.org/Nucs/2003/Rokke-Depleted-Uranium-DU21apr03.htm>. See also "Iraq: Experts Warn of Radioactive Battlefields," by Katherine Stapp, Interpress News Service, September 12, 2003. <www.ipsnews.net/interna.asp?idnews=20113> ; Scott Peterson, "Remains of Toxic Bullets Litter Iraq," *Christian Science Monitor*, May 15, 2003. <www.csmonitor.com/2003/0515/p01s02-woiq.htm>.

16. This paragraph is adapted from "The State of Civil Liberties: One Year Later, Erosion of Civil Liberties in the Post 9/11 Era," by the Center for Constitutional Rights. <www.ccr-ny.org/v2/whatsnew/report.asp?ObjID=nQdbIRkDgG& Content=153>.

17. December 5, 2003 edition, *Cigar Afficionado*. Reported, for example, in John O. Edwards, "Gen. Franks Doubts Constitution Will Survive WMD Attack," November 1, 2003. <www.newsmax.com/archives/articles/2003/11/20/185048.shtml>.

18. Fairness and Accuracy in Reporting. <www.fair.org/extra/best-of-extra/gulf-war-watch-tv.html>.

19. John Diamond, "Report Outlines Conditions for Nuclear First Strike," Associated Press, 12/08/97. <www.fas.org/news/usa/1997/12/971208-ap.htm>; Paul Reynolds, "Mini-nukes on US Agenda," August 6, 2003. <http://news.bbc.co.uk/2/hi/americas/3126141.stm>.

20. Claire Bowles, "Gamma-ray Weapons," *New Scientist*, August 13, 2003 <www.eurekalert.org/pub_releases/2003-08/ ns-gw081303.php>.

Chapter 3: Powerdown

1. For example, a study by Population Action International, "The Security Demographic: Population and Civil Conflict After the Cold War," concludes that rapid population growth and urbanization, together with land or water scarcity, seem to dramatically increase the likelihood of conflict and upheaval in poor countries. <www.populationaction.org/resources/ publi-cations/securitydemographic/download.html>.

2 Richard Dawkins, *The Selfish Gene*. Oxford University Press, 1990.

3. Ronald Bailey, *Eco-Scam: The False Prophets of Ecological Apocalypse*. St Martin's Press, 1993, p. 67.

4. Michael Sanera and Jane S. Shaw, *Facts not Fears: A Parents Guide to Teaching Kids about the Environment*. Regnery Publishing, 1996, p. 28.

5. Donnella Meadows, Dennis L. Meadows, Jorgen Randers, and William W. Behrens III, *The Limits to Growth*. Universe Books, 1972, p. 63.

6. Ibid., p. 158.

7. Ibid., p. 163.

8. Donnella Meadows, Dennis L. Meadows, and Jorgen Randers, *Beyond the Limits*. Chelsea Green, 1992; Donnella Meadows, Dennis L. Meadows, and Jorgen Randers, *The Limits to Growth: The 30-Year Update*. Chelsea Green, 2004.

9. *The Limits to Growth: The 30-Year Update*, Chelsea Green, in press.

10. Garrett Hardin, *The Immigration Dilemma: Avoiding the Tragedy of the Commons*. FAIR, 1995.

11. Richard Douthwaite, *The Growth Illusion*. New Society Publishers, 1999, p. 311.

Chapter 4: Waiting for the Magic Elixir

1. "Seabed Gas Crystal Formations Linked to Tsunami," Reuters, October 5, 2000; "Energy Ice," CBS Radio, "The Osgood File," February 22, 2001. <http://acfnewsource.org/environment/energy_ice.html>.

2. Department of Energy funding opportunity. <http://alpha.ddm.uci.edu/zotmail/archive/2003/20030926108.html>.

3. Jeremy Rifkin, *The Hydrogen Economy: The Creation of the World Wide Energy Web and the Redistribution of Power on Earth*. Tarcher/Putnam, 2002.

4. Bossel and Eliasson, "The Future of the Hydrogen Economy: Bright or Bleak." <http://planetforlife.com/h2report.pdf>.

5. Robert Sanders, "Hydrogen-Fueled Cars Not Best Way to Cut Pollution, Greenhouse Gases and Oil Dependency," UC Berkeley News, June 17, 2003. <www.mindfully.org/Energy/2003/Hydrogen-Fueled-Cars-Not17jul03.htm>. See also Joseph J. Romm, *Hype About Hydrogen: Fact and Fiction in the Race to Save the Climate*. Island Press, 2004. From a description on the publisher's web site: "Buildings and factories powered by fuel cells may indeed become common after 2010, Joseph Romm argues, but when it comes to transportation — the biggest source of greenhouse-gas emissions — hydrogen is unlikely to have a significant impact before 2050. Since the climate can't wait that long, we must act now to speed the adoption of energy-efficient and renewable energy technologies that are already commercially available. Joseph Romm, who helped run the federal government's program on hydrogen and fuel cells during the Clinton administration, provides a provocative primer on the politics, business, and technology of hydrogen and climate protection . . . . " <www.islandpress.org>.

6. Ibid.

7. *Nature*, June 13, 2003.

8. "Breakthrough in Fuel Cell Plate Technology." <www.techmonitor.net/techmon/03nov_dec/nce/nce_fuel.htm>.

9. .

10. <www.bluenergy.com/technology/beps.html>.

11. "Discovery May Spur Cheap Solar Power," CNN technology, October 2, 2003. <www.cnn.com/2003/TECH/biztech/ 10/02/solar.cells.reut/index.html>.

12. <www.postcarbon.org>.

Chapter 5: Building Lifeboats

1. Joseph Tainter, *The Collapse of Complex Societies*. Cambridge University Press, 1988; John Michael Greer, "Why Civilizations Fall: A Theory of Catabolic Collapse." Currently unpublished.

2. Joseph Tainter, "Complexity, Problem Solving, and Sustainable Societies," in Robert Constanza, ed., *Getting Down to Earth: Practical Applications of Ecological Economics*. Island Press, 1996. Archived: <http://dieoff.org/page134.htm>

3. Jared Diamond, "The Last Americans," *Harper's Magazine*, June, 2003, Vol. 306, Issue 1837.

4. Greer, op. cit.

5. John A. Hostetler, *Amish Society*. Johns Hopkins University Press, 1993.

6. Tom Brown's books (various dates) are published by Berkley Publishers Group.

7. Roberto Vacca, *The Coming Dark Age*. Doubleday, 1973.

8. Roberto Vacca, *The Death of Megalopolis*. <www.printan-dread.com/>.

9. Vacca, *The Coming Dark Age*, p. 205.

10. Ibid., pp. 200–201.

11. Ibid., p. 206.

Chapter 6: Our Choice

1. See Timothy Wilson, *Strangers to Ourselves: Discovering the Adaptive Unconscious*. Harvard University Press, 2002; Robert Wright, *The Moral Animal*. Vintage, 1994.

2. See for example, Population Action International, "The Security Demographic: Population and Civil Conflict After the Cold War." <www.populationaction.org/resources/publications/securitydemographic/>.

3. A recent exception proves the rule: in an article titled "The Numbers Game: Myths, Truths, and Half-truths About Human Population Growth and the Environment," in the January 2004 issue of *E* magazine, Jim Motavalli wrote, "There's a minefield in the American environmental movement, and its name is population. Because negotiating that minefield is so dangerous, many environmental groups and leaders have stopped trying to cross it. But to ignore population as a central issue while talking freely about sprawl, air and water pollution, loss of biodiversity, agricultural land and animal habitat, global warming and many other crucial environmental issues is to deny reality." Montavalli's article was, by its author's own admission, the first in years to address the population problem in a major environmental magazine.

INDEX

ABOUT THE AUTHOR

 RICHARD HEINBERG is a journalist, educator, lecturer, and musician. He has lectured widely, appearing on national radio and television in five countries, and is the author of five previous books, including *The Party's Over: Oil, War, and the Fate of Industrial Societies; Cloning the Buddha: The Moral Impact of Biotechnology* and *A New Covenant with Nature: Notes on the End of Civilization and the Renewal of Culture*. The latter was a recipient of the "Books to Live By" award of *Body/Mind/Spirit* magazine. He sits on the Board of Advisors of the Solar Living Institute, and on the Board of Directors of the Post Carbon Institute.

His monthly *MuseLetter* was nominated in 1994 by *Utne Reader* for an Alternative Press Award and has been included in *Utne's* annual list of Best Alternative Newsletters.

Heinberg is a member of the Core Faculty of New College of California, where he teaches courses on "Energy and Society" and "Culture, Ecology, and Sustainable Community." He is also an accomplished violinist. He and his wife, Janet Barocco, live in a suburban home they have renovated for energy efficiency, where they grow much of their own food.

If you have enjoyed *Powerdown*, you might also enjoy other

BOOKS TO BUILD A NEW SOCIETY

Our books provide positive solutions for people who
want to make a difference. We specialize in:

**Environment and Justice • Conscientious Commerce
Sustainable Living • Ecological Design and Planning
Natural Building & Appropriate Technology • New Forestry
Educational and Parenting Resources • Nonviolence
Progressive Leadership • Resistance and Community**

New Society Publishers

ENVIRONMENTAL BENEFITS STATEMENT

New Society Publishers has chosen to produce this book on recycled paper made with
100% post consumer waste, processed chlorine free, and old growth free.

For every 5,000 books printed, New Society saves the following resources:[1]

29	Trees
2,609	Pounds of Solid Waste
2,870	Gallons of Water
3,744	Kilowatt Hours of Electricity
4,742	Pounds of Greenhouse Gases
20	Pounds of HAPs, VOCs, and AOX Combined
7	Cubic Yards of Landfill Space

---

[1]Environmental benefits are calculated based on research done by the Environmental Defense Fund and
other members of the Paper Task Force who study the environmental impacts of the paper industry.

For more information on this environmental benefits statement, or to inquire about environmentally
friendly papers, please contact New Leaf Paper – info@newleafpaper.com Tel: 888 • 989 • 5323.

For a full list of NSP's titles, please call **1-800-567-6772** *or check out our web site at:*

www.newsociety.com

NEW SOCIETY PUBLISHERS